American I

An Interpret:
of Illinois

Thorne Deuel

Alpha Editions

This edition published in 2024

ISBN : 9789366388380

Design and Setting By
Alpha Editions
www.alphaedis.com
Email - info@alphaedis.com

As per information held with us this book is in Public Domain. This book is a reproduction of an important historical work. Alpha Editions uses the best technology to reproduce historical work in the same manner it was first published to preserve its original nature. Any marks or number seen are left intentionally to preserve its true form.

INTRODUCTION

This paper is primarily planned for the layman, the beginning student of prehistory and others interested in acquiring a general understanding of how primitive man lived during his successive occupations of Illinois and neighboring areas in the more important archaeological periods. Most of the archaeological data for the chief cultures or ways of life are given in references in the accompanying bibliography of technical publications selected as those from which (in the opinion of the writer) the information can be most easily gleaned.

The reconstructions given of the cultural features, where not those ordinarily inferred from archaeological findings, are based on a study of the practices commonly found among primitive people now, or until recently, living in the same stage or substage. These are tentative conclusions resulting from a study of fifty tribes in the Self-Domestication (pre-farming) stage and forty in the Plant-Raising substage. Because primitive tribes which are under pressure from people with advanced food-draft-animal agriculture or with machine industry or which are in a transitional condition between two adjacent stages are disorganized or drastically changing a formerly stabilized mode of life, great care has been exercised in drawing general conclusions from their cultural features.

The reconstructions of the perishable objects shown in the drawings are generally in keeping with the culture in which they are exhibited but cannot be vouched for as to their detailed form. The handle of an adze, the shape of a cabin roof, the headdress of a tribal chief each served the purpose for which they were made and their exact form was and is of no more consequence in the culture than the fashions in women's hats or the fins on an automobile are in our own. The details in cultures serve to set them apart from each other; it is the basic and significant features and subfeatures that determine relationships and permit the most useful classification.

The study mentioned above is still incomplete, but results so far obtained indicate:

1. That man in the same stage (and substage) of cultural development *tends* to invent and employ the same broad social and spiritual features, regardless of surroundings.

2. That where significant differences arise between substages of the same stage, they are (at least sometimes) linked with peculiarities of climate and/or natural resources which the people have seized upon and exploited to the improvement of their economic situation.

3. That many details within these broad types of economic, social and spiritual features appear to vary unpredictably within the range of available possibilities.

The stage and criterion for each were proposed in an earlier issue (No. 6) of this series, *Man's Venture In Culture*, (Deuel 1950, pp. 5-12) as:

1. *Natural Man* (*Protocultural*), when "man" presumably employed sticks and stones as implements and weapons.

2. *Self-Domestication*, following the discovery of the principle of the conchoidal fracturing of flint and its control, and the invention of tool and weapon types.

3. *Farming* or *Food-Raising*, due to the discovery that grains (grasses) and food-draft animals could be bred and raised in captivity.

4. *Inanimate Power Machine* (*Machine Age*), after the discovery of the availability of water and wind as sources for energy and the adaptation of animal-driven machines to utilize them.

Man in the wild or Protocultural stage is thought not to have reached the Americas. The oxlike mammals were not domesticated in America for drawing ploughs and vehicles, turning grain mills or to serve as a continuous food supply source. Consequently, we are concerned in the following discussion only with peoples in the Self-Domestication stage and the Plant-Raising substage of Farming.

In ordinary language, the word "culture" is used in a diversity of senses. In these pages it is used in one of two ways, the one employed being readily understood from the context. In a general sense, culture means the significant beliefs, customary activities and social prohibitions that are peculiar to man (together with the man-made tools, weapons and other material objects that he finds or has found necessary) that modify, limit or enhance in some manner, most of his discernible natural activities due to and arising from his physical animal inheritance and organization.

Culture in a specific sense refers to the significant cultural features of a group or period under consideration.

For convenience, any cultural activity according to its dominant purpose may be spoken of as belonging to one of three aspects of culture, (a) economic (technological and intellectual); (b) social (and political); and (c) spiritual (religious, artistic and recreational). To lesser degrees, most cultural activities have relationships with the two aspects other than the dominant.

Certain prevalent archaeological designations have been changed to remove time implications (e.g. "early" and "late" Woodland to *Initial* [beginning] and *Final* [end of an archaeological series]), or to shorten (e.g. "Tennessee-Cumberland" or "Gordon-Fewkes" to *Cumberland*).

Technical terms have generally been avoided; but where it has seemed necessary to retain them or to use words in a special sense, they are explained in the text or can be found in the glossary. The terms *pattern* and *phase* are those generally employed in the McKern system of classification, for the larger groupings into which it is customary to place the "cultures" as determined from the typology of the artifacts, their association in the assemblage and pertinent data recovered at a site (or local community) with due regard to circumstances of time and location of other sites nearby and over a larger area. The largest unit is the *pattern* which is made up of a number of *phases*. Cultural divisions smaller than these units are spoken of here as *subcultures*.

The approximate relationships of the archaeological units to the broader cultural stages and substages are given in Table I, page 4. The succession and coexistence of the archaeological units is indicated in the diagram "The Stream of Culture", p. 57. The summary of "Characteristics of the Archaeological-Cultural Units" occurs on pages 70-76.

This is a story mainly of Illinois when occupied by American Indians but it would not give a reasonably true picture without showing the known extensions of some of the cultures into surrounding areas and the probable intrusions from outside the state.

Of necessity in attempting a summary of the archaeology of Illinois and adjacent areas, the writer has had to lean heavily on the field work and reports of the many anthropologists who have contributed so much to the present understanding of the

American Indian in the United States. To this invaluable source material and to these able scientists the indebtedness of the writer is acknowledged to be very great indeed. In the compass of a work of this type it is impossible to name them or give them credit for original or similar views, nor is it practicable to include in the bibliography all the publications used.

Acknowledgment of assistance is made especially to Georg K. Neumann, Joseph R. Caldwell and Melvin L. Fowler, Milton D. Thompson, Ruth Kerr, Nora Deuel and Orvetta Robinson for reading and discussing the manuscript from various viewpoints, to Dr. James B. Griffin for helpful information on the dates of sites and of archaeological data, to Irvin Peithmann, Southern Illinois University, for photographs furnished, for information on sites he had discovered and the privilege of visiting them in his company, to George Langford for photographs and data regarding the Fisher site, to Charles Hodge for all photographs reproduced not otherwise credited, and to Jerry Connolly, Bettye Broyles, Barbara Parmalee and Jeanne McCarty for their excellent drawings. Without all this considerable and valuable aid the publication could not have been completed.

TABLE II. RADIOCARBON DATES[1]

CULTURAL UNIT	C14 DATE	SITE	STATE	COUNTY
MIDDLE MISSISSIPPI	A.D. 1420±200	Crable Village	Illinois	Fulton
MIDDLE MISSISSIPPI	1326±250	Nodena Village	Arkansas	Arkansas
MIDDLE MISSISSIPPI	1156±200	Cahokia	Illinois	Madison
EFFIGY MOUND[2]	1041±212	Effigy Mounds National Park	Iowa	Allamakee
HOPEWELLIAN	508±60	Twenhafel (Weber) Md.	Illinois	Jackson
HOPEWELLIAN	432±200	Rutherford Mound	Illinois	Hardin
HOPEWELLIAN	256±200	Knight Mound	Illinois	Calhoun
HOPEWELLIAN	214±250	Baehr Mound	Illinois	Brown

HOPEWELLIAN[2]	B.C. 48±160	Hopewellian Group Mound #25	Ohio	Ross
HOPEWELLIAN[3]	57±108	Wilson Mound	Illinois	White
HOPEWELLIAN	315±164	Havana Mound	Illinois	Mason
ADENA	423±150	Toepfner Mound #I	Ohio	Franklin
ADENA	697±170	Dover Mound	Kentucky	Mason
ARCHAIC	704±80	Poverty Point	Louisiana (N.E.)	W. Carroll Parish
ADENA	826±410	Toepfner Mound #II	Ohio	Franklin
ARCHAIC	904±90	Poverty Point	Louisiana (N.E.)	W. Carroll Parish
ARCHAIC	1624±300	Kays Landing	Tennessee	Humphrey
ARCHAIC[2]	2170±215	Indian Knoll	Kentucky	Ohio
ARCHAIC[2]	2360±270	Annis Mound	Kentucky	Butler
ARCHAIC	2765±300	Modoc Rock Shelter	Illinois	Randolph
ARCHAIC	2812±250	Perry Site	Alabama (N.W.)	Lauderdale
ARCHAIC	2950±250	Annis Shell Mound	Kentucky	Butler
ARCHAIC	3325±300	Modoc Rock Shelter	Illinois	Randolph
ARCHAIC	3352±300	Indian Knoll	Kentucky	Ohio
ARCHAIC	3646±400	Oconto Old Copper Site	Wisconsin (E.)	Oconto
ARCHAIC[2]	3657±164	Modoc Rock Shelter	Illinois	Randolph
ARCHAIC	5194±500	Eva Site	Tennessee	Benton
ARCHAIC	5556±400	Oconto Old Copper Site	Wisconsin (E.)	Oconto
ARCHAIC	5945±500	Graham Cave	Missouri	Montgomery
ARCHAIC	6204±300	Russell Cave	Alabama	Jackson

ARCHAIC[2]	6219±388	Modoc Rock Shelter	Illinois	Randolph
ARCHAIC	7310±352	Graham Cave	Missouri	Montgomery
ARCHAIC	7922±392	Modoc Rock Shelter	Illinois	Randolph
PALEO-INDIAN (Folsom)[2]	7934±350	Lubbock Site	Texas (N.W.)	Lubbock
PALEO-INDIAN (Sandia)	18,000	Sandia Cave	New Mexico (Center)	Bernalillo
PALEO-INDIAN (?)	22,000	Tule Spring Site	Nevada (S.E.)	Clark
PALEO-INDIAN (Clovis?)[4]	35,000	Lewisville Site	Texas	Denton

[1]These dates are selected as giving a significant picture of sequence and contemporaneity of cultures. Dates based on shell specimens are excluded on account of their general unreliability. Adena sites are not included after 400 B.C. These are burial mounds and with their inferred customs may be present in two or more cultural units rather than constitute a feature characteristic of one.

[2]An average of at least two dates for this period.

[3]Average of three out of four dates. Libby's second date disregarded as widely out of line.

[4]Two samples gave identical results. Cultural identification as Clovis based on single spearhead is doubtful.

PALEO-INDIANS, BIG GAME HUNTERS, DISCOVER A NEW WORLD (50,000? to 8,000? B.C.)[5]

Man probably discovered America as early as 50,000 years ago and gradually occupied the two continents in the succeeding millenia. The first discoverers of the New World were of Mongolian racial stock as are the American Indians. They crossed from Siberia to Alaska over an existing land bridge, over ice, or possibly by wading or by boat over the shallow sea in the wake of mammoth, mastodon or musk ox herds on whose flesh they lived. Following in the path of the huge animals, they made their way possibly up the Yukon from its mouth to the divide, thence down into the Mackenzie Basin, and along a great river where now exist a chain of lakes and so into the Mississippi Valley.

The migrants trailing each herd doubtless traveled in their several ways in family groups, uniting from time to time to trap and kill one of the great shaggy beasts. When the animals stopped, the families bedded down nearby in the most sheltered spots available taking care not to lose touch with the herd. These were wanderers, not explorers, nor were they seeking new homes; they were hunters that traveled where the herd led.

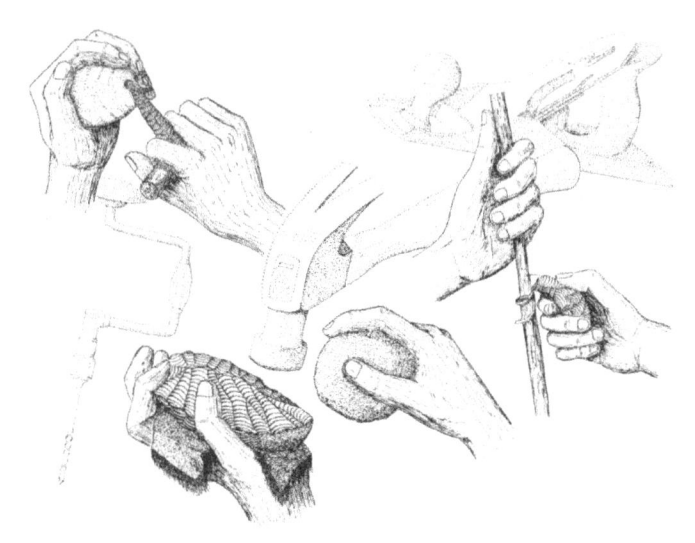

Fig. 1. Archaic flint drill, stone hammer, and flint scraper as used in Archaic period and their modern steel counterparts. (B.B.)

Fig. 2. Paleo-Indians attack a mired-down mammoth. (B.G.P.)

Fig. 3. Paleo-Indian spearheads from the William Small collection. A, B, and C are Clovis points; D, a Folsom point. All are from Illinois.

Their belongings, by our standards, were pitifully few, their way of life laborious, full of hardship and danger, but their needs were simple and their means of meeting them doubtless seemed ample to these hardy hunters. The chief weapon was a thrusting spear with a chipped flint head and a long shaft to keep the hunter as far from harm's way as possible when attacking the dangerous animal. The narrow width of the spearpoint made it easy to withdraw from a wound and attack again. Our evidence that the

Paleo-Indians (as the Big Game Hunters are commonly called) lived in Illinois are these same spearheads (Clovis and Folsom types), usually grooved or fluted lengthwise of the blade, which are scattered over much of the Illinois prairie as isolated finds. No campsites of this people have yet been discovered in Illinois, as they have been in Pennsylvania, Alabama and several southwestern states. We can only surmise that in Illinois the hunters also had stone hammers and chipped flint scrapers as they had elsewhere.

Having arrived in the great central valley between the Rocky Mountains and the eastern ranges, the herds probably moved slowly from one browsing ground to another in the open corridor between glaciers. It may have taken them many years to reach what is now the United States. Eventually the herds wandered back and forth across the Mississippi Valley, and some favorable spots came to be used as camping grounds again and again by the same or different families. Such places would appeal immediately to the campers because of their protection from rain and the piercing glacial winds, the presence of a plentiful supply of wood and water. The possibility of our gaining a better knowledge of Paleo-Indian life in Illinois rests on the discovery of such a site, difficult now to recognize because it may no longer provide wood, water, or shelter of any sort.

There are in southern Illinois a number of simple linear stone piles known locally as "stone forts," all in the same type of land structure. Each forms an obstruction five to fifteen feet in height across a narrow neck or ridge leading to the plateau top of a near-vertical-sided "promontory" projecting out into a stream valley, making an excellent corral, with no fence necessary except across the entrance. They may have been used in late Paleo-Indian times and on into the Archaic period for impounding large game and/or driving them over the cliff.

ARCHAIC MAN, FIRST SETTLER IN ILLINOIS (8000 to 2500 B.C.)[6]

We have reason to believe that the Big Game Hunters wandered over Illinois and the adjoining states during the last advance of the glaciers. Around 12,000 B.C. the climate in the Midwest became milder, the glaciers "retreated," and the mighty torrents—the Mississippi, the Ohio and the Illinois that had torn irresistibly down their valleys—shrank into smaller, less turbulent rivers that occupied but a fraction of their former beds. The great shaggy mammoths, musk oxen, the ground sloths and the giant beavers moved westward toward the mountains or to the north.

Some of the Big Game Hunters with their families may have followed the retreating glacier and the herds; others stayed behind in country to which they had grown attached. With the great herds gone, the human families remaining in Illinois had to hunt the game animals that now frequented the area—deer, elk (wapiti), bear and smaller mammals. The large hunting party was no longer practicable. The game roamed over the country singly or by twos or threes and had to be stalked by one or two hunters. Families were compelled to live widely separated one from another in order to secure ample food throughout the year. Thus developed a new way of life which we call the Archaic phase or culture.

The hunter, as time passed, learned the secret habits of the deer, bear and raccoon and the more sluggish fishes. His wife and daughters learned the haunts and ways of the smaller animals, the rodents, turtles and lizards, discovered where edible greens, wild tubers, nuts and fruits grew and where mussels and snails abounded in creeks and rivers. With increasing knowledge Archaic man made better and fuller use of his changed and changing surroundings, food became more plentifully available, life easier and less hazardous though still very difficult from our standpoint.

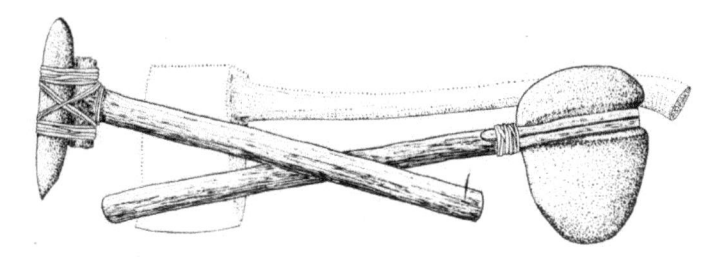

Fig. 4. Hafted primitive stone adze and grooved ax, with modern steel-bitted ax in the background. (B.B.)

With new needs and some leisure from the labor of providing food, Archaic man invented specialized devices, new methods of making tools and weapons, the more skillful among them shaping the objects carefully into symmetrical forms pleasing to the eye of others and strangely satisfying to the maker.[7] He pecked a hollow in both sides of his cobblestone hammer so he could grip it securely and use it more skillfully. He pecked and ground diorite and granite into adzes, hatchets (celts), and axes with a groove for hafting. These were a decided improvement over flaked choppers. He ground and polished banded and highly-colored shale ("slate") into prismatic and cylindrical spearthrower weights and bored them with a tube, sand and water. His own person he decked out with necklaces and oval pendants (made by boring a hole in smooth flat waterworn pebbles) and with bone ornaments cut to shape, ground, engraved and polished. These he and his wife wore as had their forefathers but not the skin robes of glacial times.

As life grew easier, the family or local group increased in size. Sons brought their wives to the family dwelling place and built windbreaks near those of their parents. With food abundant the little settlement became a small cluster of households or a hamlet consisting possibly of sixty to seventy persons.

If Archaic Man Was Like Present-Day Archaic Tribes[8]

Fig. 5. Rock shelter near Cobden. Such shelters were used by Archaic and succeeding peoples. (Photograph by Irvin Peithmann)

If Archaic man in Illinois lived as do present-day Archaic peoples, the family or local group, though they restricted themselves during most of the year to their hunting grounds which they guarded jealously from trespassers, did not camp continuously in one spot. At appropriate seasons of the year they rotated from one hamlet site to another to take advantage of the food resources of that locality. In winter perhaps they moved to a rock shelter, like that of Modoc in Randolph County, Illinois, near the wooded valleys of streams emptying into the river where deer and elk sought protection from the rigors of winter; in spring to upland lakes for duck and other waterfowl; and in autumn to wooded parklands to harvest acorns, hickory nuts, and berries. The spot chosen for each hamlet location was generally one that had been so used at that same season from time out of mind by the family and its forebears.

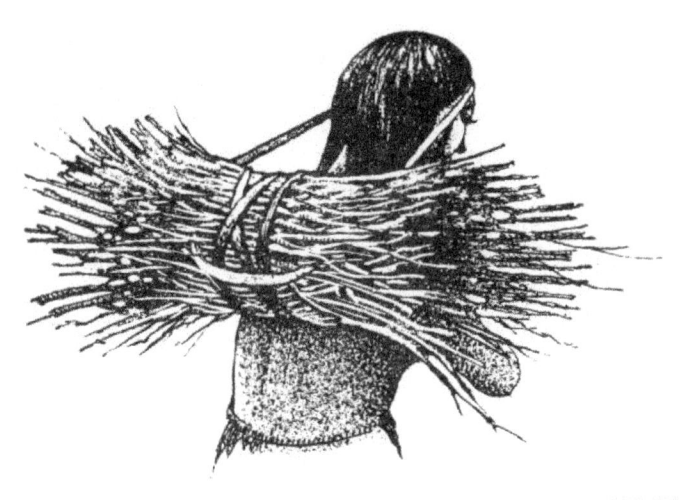

Fig. 6. Primitive woman carrying a load with the aid of a tumpline. (J.C.)

It is probable, as among most primitive peoples, that men did only work thought suitable to men, and women that appropriate for women. Men made the weapons and tools they used, did the hunting and fishing, and the fighting (when quarrels developed into feuds or wars between local groups of the same tribe). The rest of the labor fell to the women—caring for the children, collecting edible plants, clams and small animals, preparing the food, and carrying burdens. All work was done by hand; loads were carried on the back. It is possible that boats, perhaps of dugout type, were used as among present-day Archaic peoples living on waterways. There was no other specialization and each "household" provided for the needs of all its members to the best of its ability. No food was grown and no domestic animal except the dog was known.

Once or twice a year when food was easily and bountifully available, local groups from nearby hunting territories met together for religious rites. These local groups spoke the same dialect, had the same way of life, and considered themselves a unit or tribe. They had no political form of government but were kept in order through habits formed by early training and by extension of the kinship system to the whole tribe. Thus the tribal elders were considered fathers and mothers, and to them were due obedience and respect, just as children they had been taught to regard their own blood fathers, uncles, and other older relatives.

The elders knew the tribal customs; and to be accepted as a tribal member, boys must respect, learn and conform to these customs.

The object of these annual gatherings was to teach the young the tribal customs and to perform solemn ceremonies, the purpose of which was to insure the security and well-being of the tribe, a continuing abundance of the favorite foods, and to express gratitude and thanksgiving to unseen Spirits who watched over the game animals (and possibly the edible plants) for the blessings received during the past year. These gatherings and cooperative undertakings served, on the one hand, as a welcome change from the usual daily grind and afforded opportunities for the young to get acquainted and choose mates and, on the other, to unify the language and customs of the constituent local groups, to enhance the influence of the tribal elders and keep fresh in the minds of all the history of the tribe, the importance of its activities, and its sacred tradition, all essential to the way of life of dynamic Archaic peoples of recent times.

Fig. 7. Fertility rites were probably performed by Archaic peoples to ensure the abundance of game animals for the next year. (J.C.)

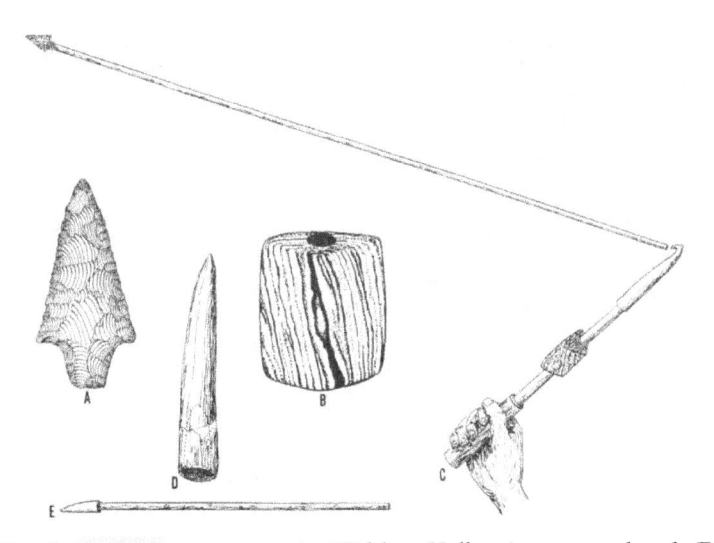

Fig. 8. Archaic weapons: A, Hidden Valley type spearhead; B, prismatic atlatl weight of polished red shale; C, throwing a spear with an atlatl; D, socketed antler spearhead; E, short thrusting spear or javelin. A, B, and D are from Modoc Shelter in Randolph County, Illinois.

In the later (Medial) Archaic period at Modoc, the dead were buried in the floor of the rock shelter. Burial probably indicates a belief in life after death. Care in preparing the body for burial, in the funeral rites and burying, and in the customary mourning thereafter was highly important so the dead man could go promptly to the spirit world in peace and not remain in the neighborhood to disturb his kinsmen. Immediately after the burial, it is probable that the little settlement removed to a distant location as is customary with peoples in this stage of culture.

The rites for important dead in the Terminal period probably began with the conventional mourning of relatives, with painting the body with red ochre and grease and adorning it with the dead man's jewelry, followed at the appropriate time by the conveyance of the body to the grave side, where the corpse was deposited in a pit together with personal insigne and weapons. The grooved stone axe, large spearheads, daggers, bannerstones, spearthrower with weight and more rarely copper articles were placed alongside or on the corpse. In some instances large stones were laid upon the grave probably for one or more of the following reasons: (a) to mark the grave of an important tribesman; (b) to keep the body from being disturbed by animals; and (c) to hold the dead man's ghost until he departed for the spirit world.

Fig. 9. Grooved stone axes are frequently found in Archaic graves but were not buried with the dead after this period. (J.C.)

It is very probable that, on occasions of social and religious import, Modoc man and other Archaic tribes in Illinois bedecked themselves in their best paint and jewelry. Possibly the colorful and intriguing bannerstones, which were undoubtedly developed from the spearthrower weight, were carried or worn by the local group headmen who had won that right because they were skillful hunters, courageous fighters, or learned in the tribal customs and beliefs and thus recognized by the tribe as leaders for the time being.

Fig. 10. Anculosa shell necklace with flat pendant of water-worn stone from the Archaic period. Anculosa necklaces were worn by many Illinois peoples probably up to the European contact period.

CULTURES AND CULTURAL CHANGE

Man can live virtually anywhere on the earth's surface where he can obtain food, water and fuel, and do so without any fundamental change in his physical structure. This is largely because he is easily able to modify his customary ways of filling his basic needs under new or changing conditions of his surroundings. For primitive man to "live better" required an increasing knowledge of the resources in his locality and ingenuity in devising effective means and contrivances for exploiting them.

Because of this ability, the Paleo-Indian wanderers (Big Game Hunters) in Illinois around 12,000 to 10,000 B.C., when confronted with rising temperatures and other regional changes, could choose whether they would follow the mammoth and musk ox herds and familiar subglacial conditions elsewhere or adopt new and strange methods of securing food and other requirements.

As Big Game Hunters they probably lived as a number of families attached to a herd and relatively independent of each other except at hunting times. They had no homes, only temporary camps, and were bound to a moving herd, not to any particular region. The Paleo-Indian culture consisted of methods of trapping and slaying the great beasts and of filling other simple physical needs; a simple code of social behavior which enabled men and wives to live together with their children and, for brief periods, in gatherings of the families in relative peace and contentment; with religious beliefs and rites suitable to their cultural level that they believed assured them of a continuance of their satisfactory existence.

When the climate changed, those families that chose to remain in Illinois had to develop, perhaps slowly and painfully, a new way of life. The habits and haunts of deer, elk, bear and raccoon had to be learned. Other methods of hunting and of making tools and devices to fit new conditions were invented as a result of the new fund of knowledge assembled. Each family eventually acquired a more or less definite piece of land or hunting territory in which it selected certain favorable places to build the temporary hamlet at suitable seasons. As the man and his family became better adapted to the land and its resources, he hunted more successfully, and the family or local group grew larger in number.

Probably a number of neighboring families, when food was especially abundant, gathered together for social and religious purposes as peoples living today in the same status still do. Religious beliefs and other customs had all this time doubtless been shifting gradually in meeting the needs and dangers of changing conditions to a new way of life we call the Archaic culture.

Every way of life is built on an older, often simpler, culture from which it has changed more or less rapidly. Due to important inventions, the group may modify its economy (ways of securing and processing food, etc.) and produce a substantially improved manner of living which, from archaeological evidence alone, may be difficult to recognize as a development from its earlier phase.

On occasion, people from another region may invade an area, drive out the inhabitants and bring in a differing way of life. Usually this merely extends, to a desirable region less effectively exploited by others, the range of a vigorous cultural group whose territory has become too densely populated.

Sometimes newcomers essay to live peaceably with the natives and a new cultural blend is developed. If fundamental changes are made in the economy by internal development or by imitating another culture, social and religious customs are very likely to change too, though usually at a slower pace.

As time went on, the Archaic way of life slowly changed and finally disappeared, but probably not so suddenly as might at first appear; for many Archaic customs, tools, and weapons continued to be made and used in the "new" culture by the descendants of rugged earlier people or were adopted by newcomers to the region. Other changes were added through new inventions and incoming people from other regions producing a new culture now generally known as Woodland.

THE INITIAL WOODLAND CULTURES[9]
(2500-500 B.C.)

After 5000 B.C. the temperatures continued to rise producing a climatic interval known as the Thermal Maximum when it was warmer and drier than at the present time. After reaching its high point, the temperature gradually declined and probably ended in southern Illinois about 2100 B.C. or later in a climate much like that of today.

By projecting the rate of deposit from the eight- to the eleven-foot level of the Modoc Rock Shelter up to the five-foot level where the Archaic remains appear to end, we secure a date for its upper limit of about 2100 B.C. (Deuel 1957, p. 2). The remains between the five- and eight-foot depths are scantier and less varied than in the earlier (lower) layers and may indicate a cultural group in a losing struggle to maintain itself under changing conditions.

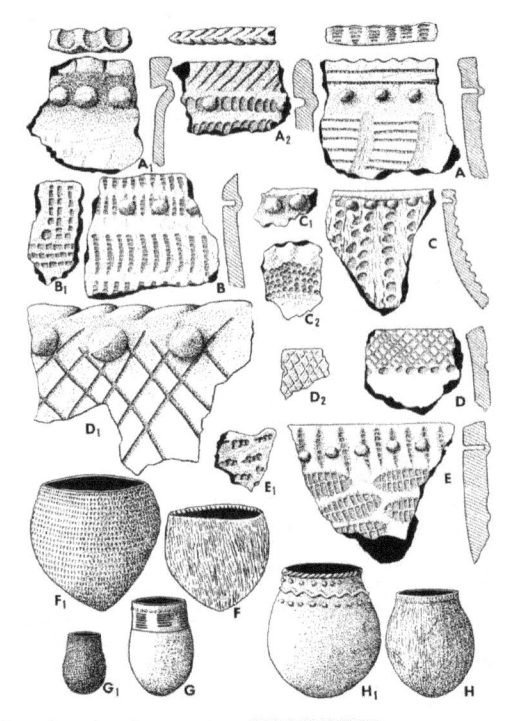

Fig. 11. Potsherds from the Lake Baikal in southern Siberia resemble those of Initial and Classic Woodland (Hopewellian) in

Illinois. The letters with subscripts refer to Siberian pottery. A-E, reduced to ½ actual size; F-H, reduced to $1/16$ actual size. (Siberian pottery from Richthofen in ANTHROPOS, 1932: 128, 129, 130; Illinois pottery from Illinois State Museum collections.)

In northern Illinois, similar climatic conditions were developing. There, possibly as early as 2500 B.C., a new culture, the Initial (early) Woodland, was coming into existence. At any rate, groups living there some time prior to 1000 B.C. made pottery, placed their dead in cemeteries and in low burial mounds in a flexed or "doubled-up" position, occasionally with food, personal ornaments and other funeral offerings.

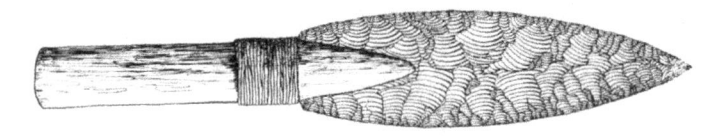

Fig. 12. A flint dagger or hunting knife from "Red Ochre subculture" of Initial Woodland. (B.B.)

The pottery of one Woodland group (Morton) in the Illinois valley resembled, in shape, surface treatment, design and area decorated, pots made in the Lake Baikal region in Asia some 7000 miles distant. The appearance of such striking similarities has long been a puzzle to anthropologists. In the first place the detailed likenesses suggest both were made by one and the same people. It seems fairly obvious that the several resemblances did not travel from tribe to tribe from Asia to central North America. The preservation of a pottery tradition during a migration of 7000 miles, probably lasting for several generations, seems equally incredible. Perhaps the most plausible explanation is that two widely separated divisions of a people originating in central Asia with the same cultural background and similar surroundings arrived independently at a remarkably similar but very simple pottery type.

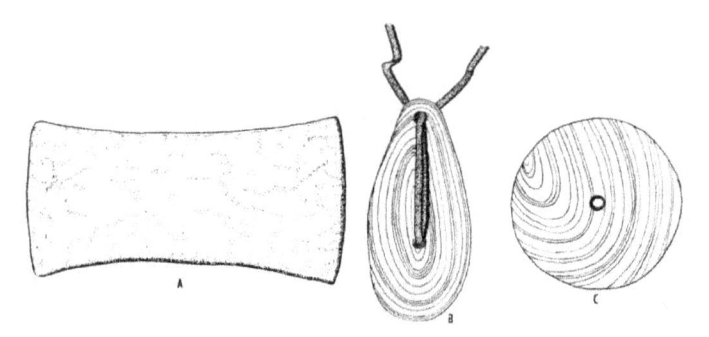

Fig. 13. A copper gorget, A, (possibly patterned after the double-bitted ax-shaped bannerstone) and shell gorgets, B and C, from "Red Ochre subculture" of Initial Woodland. All from Mound 11, Fulton County, Illinois.

These late migrants probably found groups like the Black Sand (and Red Ochre) peoples in Illinois who were just emerging from the Archaic phase into Initial Woodland. The settlements of all early Woodland peoples were small in extent and poor in cultural remains. The population of these hamlets probably seldom exceeded fifty. No traces of house structures have yet been discerned. Temporary huts, probably built of small poles and brush, may have been conical or hemispherical in shape. The artifacts or cultural objects, except for a small amount of jewelry (shell and copper beads and pendants) and the few offerings placed in graves, show little evidence of any urge to fine workmanship or much feeling for beauty of line or form. Life was probably too hard and the effort in securing food and other requirements too exacting to leave much leisure for artistic workmanship in durable materials.[10]

THE FOOD STORERS (BAUMER AND CRAB ORCHARD CULTURES) (1000?-100 B.C.?)

It has been seen that in southern Illinois the Archaic way of life may have persisted until 2100 B.C. or perhaps even later. Across the state on the Ohio River a Woodland people succeeded the earlier Archaic residents. Their culture is known as Baumer and their nearest cultural relatives lived south of the Ohio in Kentucky (Round Grave or Upper Valley People). The Baumer artifacts do not resemble those of the Archaic period very closely, giving one the impression that the Baumer people developed their way of life elsewhere and moved into Illinois, possibly while Archaic groups were still in the region.

The Baumer culture differs in several ways from the northern Initial Woodland; actually it appears to be more advanced although it has been termed early Woodland by some archaeologists. In the first place, the area of settlement was more extensive which seems to indicate a larger population than do early northern Woodland campsites. Their artifacts are numerous and varied, suggesting they were well adapted to their surroundings. Flat forms of polished stone (resembling in outline certain Archaic bannerstones from which they may have derived) served presumably as breast ornaments or gorgets (as similar pieces did in the Hopewellian period). Tear-shaped stone objects (plummets) were made as they had been in Medial and Terminal Archaic. House structures were semi-permanent, large, square, made of poles or logs set in holes in the ground. Huts with circular floors seem to have been in use also. Most important of the cultural habits noted were numerous pits apparently for the storage of food. In these the remains of acorns and hickory nuts were found. These people, like the acorn gatherers of California and the Eskimo, knew how to preserve food over long periods. Acorns were probably abundant enough for a Baumer family to lay up several months' supply in a short time. This permitted them to live in larger settlements and gave them sufficient leisure to build rather substantial houses and shape symmetrical ornaments from stone. These facts seem to substantiate the hypothesis that they were a sedentary people by virtue of their knowledge of how to store food.

Fig. 14. Housewife storing roasted acorns in a pit near door of her square log cabin dwelling. Characteristic clay vessel ("flowerpot" type) with "mat-impressed exterior." Baumer period. (J.C.)

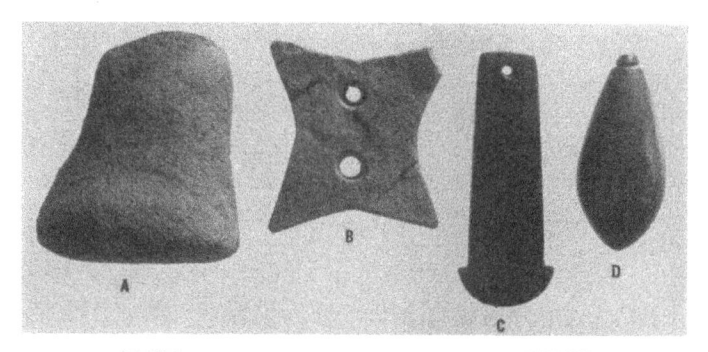

Fig. 15. A, stone pestle; B, reel-shaped stone gorget; C, "spud-shaped" stone gorget or pendant; D, grooved plummet. From the Baumer subculture and site.

Fig. 16. Pots from the Crab Orchard period of Baumer subculture recovered from the Sugar Camp Hill Site by Moreau Maxwell for Southern Illinois University. Vessel in center is roughly 16" tall. (Photographs furnished through courtesy of Dr. James B. Griffin, Univ. of Michigan.)

The size of the Baumer settlement, the semi-permanent houses, the presence of chipped spades, stone pestles and pottery might lead one to think that these people were plant-growers rather than simple food storers. Comparing them with the acorn-gathering tribes of California, who were storers and not food growers, it is seen that these, too, had permanent settlements with well over one hundred inhabitants, rather substantial houses, stone pestles, and some tribes, at least, had pottery vessels. The Californians doubtless had digging tools since the rooms of some houses were dug four feet down into the soil.

Traces of Hopewellian influence, possibly indicating inter-marriage with Hopewellians, have been noted at the Sugar Camp Hill site (date undetermined) in Jackson County, which is presumably later than Baumer. However, the Baumerians like the native Californians were conservative, for four centuries intervened between the oldest Hopewellian village in the north and the earliest known station of that culture in southern Illinois.[11]

THE HOPEWELLIAN CIVILIZATION[12] (500 B.C.-500 A.D.)

Toward the end of the Initial Woodland period maize or corn, as we call it today, was introduced into northern Illinois, presumably from Mexico and Middle America through the agency of intervening tribes. In an apparently short time, its production seems to have been greatly intensified and exploited. Other food crops and tobacco may have accompanied maize.

About the same time, a formalized religion arose, probably concerned with the worship of deities who personified natural forces like the sun, rain and thunder, which were important to a plant-growing people. From the evidence of burial places, there seem to have been two or possibly three social classes. Doubtless the first comprised the families who introduced and grew the new food plants and who were inspired to invent the complex religion. The burial of the dead, especially those socially important and of the highest class, was accompanied by elaborate and colorful ceremonies closely bound to the religion. This seems to be a continuation in grander form of the earlier Red Ochre funeral and burial. It is unfortunate that we do not have tangible evidence of their other religious and political ceremonies which may have been even more impressive and significant. The official dress and insignia of the officials, which we can barely glimpse in the rich and varied remains in the tombs, signify a political system of social control and an established priesthood for the spiritual guidance of the community. Shamans or medicine men probably had only the duty of treating disease. Reverence for and possibly worship of ancestors is suggested by the impressive tomb chambers and mounds and the care obviously bestowed on certain of their socially prominent dead.

Social and political prestige, religious pomp and ceremonial, all seem to have combined to stimulate a demand for rare materials, beautiful jewels and impressive regalia. This initiated the search for pearls at home, the development of skillful and artistic workmanship in flint, bone, shell, copper and mica, travel abroad and trade in materials obtainable only in distant regions.

Aside from those technologies connected with the growing of plant foods, probably few new crafts appeared in the culture; rather those already, existing in the Initial Woodland were raised to a high degree of excellence. Art in several forms flourished—

carving in the round and in relief, the making of fine symmetrical polished, decorated and painted pottery commonly called typical Hopewellian, hammered copper jewelry, the setting of pearls and highly-colored native stones as eyes in sculptured animals and in bear-tooth pendants and ear ornaments, etching of delicate designs, naturalistic and conventional, on bone and the modeling and firing of exquisite statuettes in clay. We admire and wonder at the excellence of execution in the best of their small sculpture because they are skillfully fashioned and finished and because they so accurately portray the characteristics and habits of animals with which we are familiar. The artist had the crudest of tools to aid him—rough stone hammers and an anvil for pecking stone to the general form; sandstone files or abraders; clay and water to polish pieces; flint and tubular drills for boring; and flint knives to cut and engrave pottery and bone—in spite of which the best craftsmen well knew how to bring out the beauty of the piece.

Fig. 17. Artist's idea of a Hopewellian chief or high priest in full ceremonial regalia. (J.C.) Evidence for dress (except for calumet) has been found in Illinois.

For the first time in Amerindian history in Illinois we become aware of an accumulation of wealth, a surplus of handmade goods over and above those needed for survival; many of these were neither well-suited nor intended for immediate physical needs, but rather were aimed at social display or spiritual enhancement. Wealth reflects a relatively constant and abundant supply of food and other necessities and the resulting accompaniment of considerable leisure time for a sizable portion of the community. It may also mark the beginning of craft specialization.[13]

It is hardly necessary to add that, if such a profusion of grave offerings as indicated by Hopewellian tombs—feather cloth robes, pearl necklaces, copper hatchets, and beautifully fashioned art objects—were left with the dead, that the high political and religious officers were correspondingly bedecked in gorgeous apparel for civil and religious ceremonies.

Nor should sight be lost of the fact that these creations and materials, so commonplace and inexpensive today, were to the Hopewellians as valuable and highly desirable as gold, silk, and precious stones are to us in Western civilization. For a better perspective these tomb offerings should be compared with objects usually found in camp and grave sites of the Initial and Final Woodland peoples.

Traders may have gone to distant regions to select and barter for raw materials, to the Lake Superior region for copper, to Ohio for pipestone, to the south Atlantic and Gulf Coasts for the small Marginella and Oliva shells, for the larger Cassis and Busycon shells, and to the Yellowstone or Mexico for obsidian (of which little is found in Illinois graves). Trade, to some degree, removes the limitations imposed by the immediate surroundings. Pearls were secured in quantity from the clams of the native streams. Bone, antler, tortoise and clam shell, bears' teeth, bear, wildcat and wolverine jaws from their hunting and collecting pursuits were utilized more fully than ever before. Even human jaws, possibly of enemies, were cut, polished and bored for use as pendants.

Though the Hopewellians may not have been the pacifists they are sometimes painted, there must have been long periods of peaceful relationships with distant and nearer neighbors with whom they traded or through whose territories their traders had to pass. Whether or not a condition of peace was maintained within the borders of their culture area by the force of arms is an interesting question that cannot now be answered.

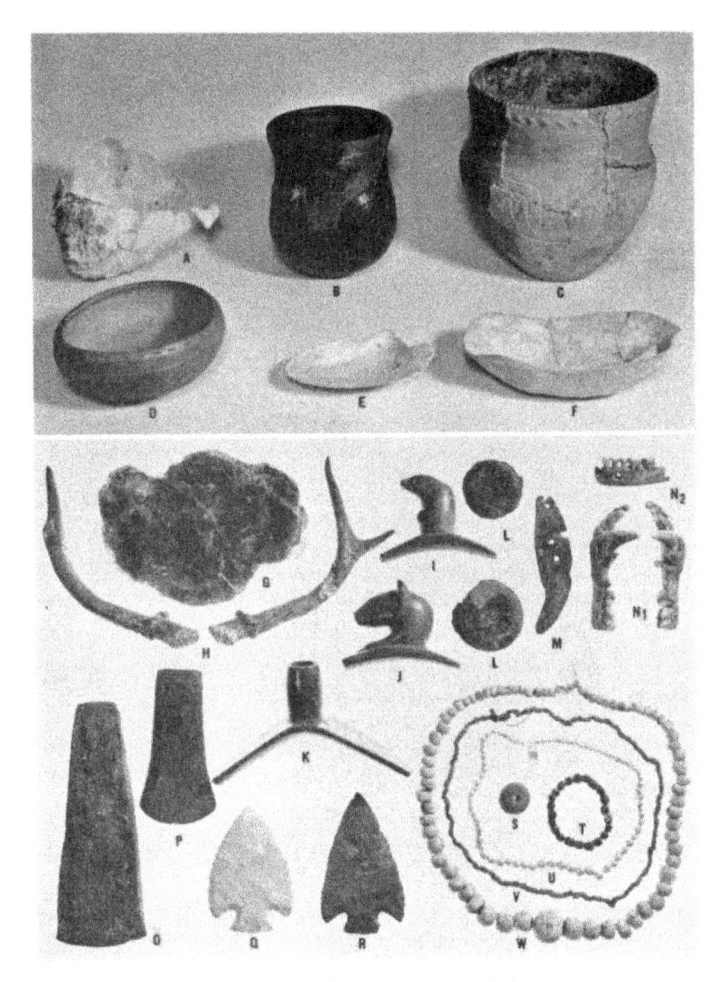

Fig. 18. The Hopewellian assemblage of artifacts that collectively identify the Hopewellian (Classic Woodland) period and, except for shell spoon, turtle shell dish, and some bead types, distinguish it from the other Woodland assemblages. A, drinking cup of marine shell (*Cassis madagascarensis*); B, C, D, Hopewellian pottery (restored); E, mussel shell spoon with "handle"; F, turtle shell dish; G, sheet mica (mirror?); H, antler headdress; I, J, platform pipes with effigy mammal bowls, polished stone (Otter and bear's head, eyes set with copper pellets); K, platform pipe (plain bowl), curved base, polished stone; L, copper earspools or ornaments,

pair; M, imitation bear tooth, copper; N, (Below) N₁, Bear jaw, cut in half, ground and drilled to be worn as a double pendant; (Above) N₂, Fragment of a human jaw that has been similarly treated; O, copper hatchet that carries imprint of textile on its surface; P, copper adze; Q, R, Hopewellian spearheads; S, massive bead of copper; T, bracelet of copper beads; U, necklace of pearls; V, necklace of copper beads; W, necklace of graduated ground shell beads from columella (central column) of marine shell.

In southern Illinois the advance of Hopewellian culture was slower. The infiltration of new pottery styles noted at Crab Orchard very possibly represents intermarriage with Hopewellian women. Possibly through ties of relationship and the acceptance of the new food plants, the old Baumer way of life was submerged by the Hopewellian customs though here and there former habits still are recognizable. Some customs of Baumer and Crab Orchard were adopted by the northern Hopewellians—the reel-shaped gorget, the plummet and the chipped stone hoe.

In the north of Illinois, Hopewellian lasted until 250 A.D. (Poole site) and in the west and south to about 450 or 500 A.D. Though the culture died out in Illinois by 500 A.D., it still flourished in Mississippi (Bynum site) around 800 A.D. and at Marksville, Louisiana, as late as 850 A.D.

As was stated earlier, emerging cultures grow out of earlier ones. Although it may not yet be generally recognized, the Hopewellian civilization probably exerted tremendous influence on the Mississippi cultures and on tribes that followed them in the great central valley of the United States and beyond, down to historic times. It must be borne in mind that in spite of their splendid achievements, the Hopewellians had no domestic animals but the dog, no herds for meat and great wealth, no draft animals to drag the plough and turn the mill. All labor was "by hand," all transport on the back or in a boat driven by human power.

THE DARK AGE IN ILLINOIS—FINAL
WOODLAND (200 to 900 A.D.)

The Hopewellian civilization apparently disappeared as suddenly as it seems to have arisen. This impression is probably due to the fact that the people continued to live in the old villages long after the characteristic colorful Hopewell customs were no longer practiced. Actually the culture may have declined for a century or more before it finally broke down completely. Many of the simpler folk traditions probably persisted in the area for some centuries afterward.

Possibly long continued abuses of power and privilege by religious and political officials, especially those from the highest social caste, weakened the confidence of the lower classes in their leaders and the culture. Newcomers from Iowa, Missouri and Kentucky may have further disorganized certain settlements and separated areas of the larger community from each other. Generally, however, the writer gets the impression that the decay began within the civilization although its final downfall may have been accelerated by external pressures.

With failing confidence and a rising uneasiness, trade would naturally decrease and the incentive to fine workmanship decline. The larger cultural community split apart into a number of small tribes, who were isolationists and individualists. All the separate little tribal units were Woodland culturally with some small evidence of their Hopewellian heritage, but each differed in certain respects from its neighbors. Villages dwindled to the mere hamlets, widely separated one from another. The elaborate ceremonial dress, insignia, and jewelry, and the artistic creations (at least in durable materials) became a part of the past; the people found themselves reduced to the rude cultural level of their early Woodland ancestors. Huts were flimsy and left no discernible remains. Tools, weapons, and ornaments were, in general, carelessly made and poorly finished. Although tobacco was smoked and small patches of maize and beans may have been grown, the chief economic dependence undoubtedly was on hunting, fishing and collecting.

Fig. 19. Group of mounds exhibiting bird, mammal, linear and conical mounds as they occur characteristically in Effigy Mound subculture of Final Woodland. (B.B.)

The religious beliefs, too, were probably simplified and mixed with magic and superstition, surviving relics of the religion of the past age. In a word, the social and religious customs of the little tribes were broadly similar but in minor details differed from each other much as do their artifactual remains.

A study of the Final Woodland and other phases of Illinois history reveals certain relationships among some distinguishable differences of detail:

1. The almost complete lack of evidence of Hopewellian art, trade and religion in the late Woodland period gives little apparent indication that the people were the direct descendants and heirs of that civilization. On the other hand, the general resemblance of Final Woodland assemblages to those of the Initial phase seems marked. Let us examine further.

Fig. 20. Graves near Quincy, Illinois, Stone Vault period. (Photographs through courtesy of O. D. Thurber.)

Stone mound after earth was removed.

Four excavated "vaults", the third of which shows a "corridor" entrance with stone steps.

The tobacco pipe of the late phase with the stem projecting beyond the bowl is found in most aspects. Likewise, the vertically

- 33 -

elongated pot is common but not the only form. Burials are often in mounds, frequently in a central chamber or grave, with skeletons in the flexed and/or extended positions, occasionally accompanied by grave offerings. All these are broadly reminiscent of Hopewellian customs and, in the writer's opinion, indicate a continuing thread of tradition from Initial Woodland through Hopewellian into the Final phase.

2. The relationship to the Middle Mississippi seems more evident and has been attributed by some authors to the "impact" of a high culture on that of cruder or "under-developed" neighbors. What are the grounds for these conclusions?

New pottery forms were being attempted, the flattened globular pot, the shallow bowl (occasionally found in Hopewellian sites), the cup or beaker and the plate. In southern counties, a new method of making pits is indicated by a tendency of sherds, even grit-tempered ones, to split or laminate (see Maxwell, *Woodland Cultures of Southern Illinois*, Beloit, 1951, p. 204). Secondary features previously lacking begin to appear as "raised points" or knobs on rims, some roughly resembling animal heads with ears and a snout. Triangular arrowheads and others reflecting larger spearhead types are all made from curved, not flat flakes as the Mississippian points are. The stone discoidal that seems to be the game piece of the historically known chunkey game, which was possibly initiated in late Hopewellian times (see Fowler, *The Rutherford Mound*, Springfield, 1957, pp. 31-33) occurs in the Bluff subculture and probably in the Tampico also.

Fig. 21. Canton ware pot (Tampico subculture) from Clear Lake village site in Tazewell County. Designs are formed with cord impressions. (From Schoenbeck collection in Illinois State Museum. Max. diam. at shoulder 18".

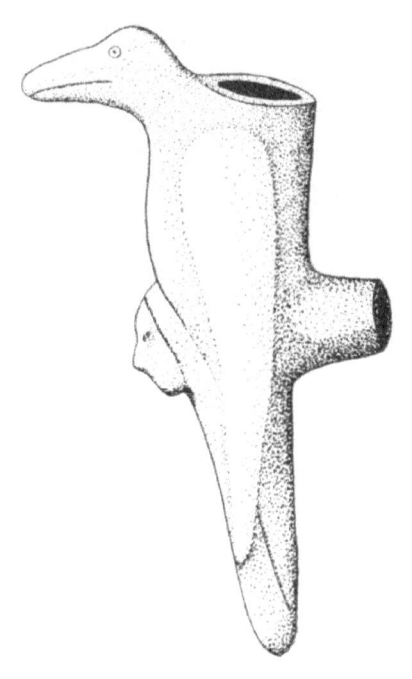

Fig. 22. "Handled" pipe in form of raven with head projecting from rim, from Jersey Bluff subculture. After Titterington. Reduced about ½.

All these bespeak Middle Mississippian tendencies. A common conclusion, as mentioned previously, is that these features were borrowed from non-Woodland groups. The writer, however, gets the impression from his studies that the Middle Mississippi phase developed through the interplay of invention and adoption of improvements, modification and re-invention, between the Final Woodland subcultures in Illinois and adjacent territory. This does not mean that Illinois communities alone were responsible for the emergence of this phase but rather that they played an important dynamic role in its development. The Cahokia subculture of western and central Illinois probably constituted the native local tribe or nation.

Final Woodland Archaeology

Archaeologically these peoples are in the Final Woodland phase of culture. The Final Phase yields tobacco pipes and crude flint arrowheads, its chief artifactual differences with the Initial phase. The clay of their pottery was generally mixed with grit or sand to prevent firing cracks in the vessel walls. The customary vertically-elongated pot with a conical or pointed bottom was accompanied by new forms—the globular or flattened globular with "round" (spherical) bases, the "coconut shell" cup or larger vessel, and shallow bowls. The flattened globular pots and the bowls were occasionally decorated with two or four knobs or with "raised points" on the rim, sometimes giving a squarish appearance to the mouth. In some instances these decorative projections were crudely modeled ears and snout which give the effect of animals' heads facing out and foreshadowing the Middle Mississippi effigy shallow bowls. An important invention, the bow and arrow, appears in Illinois for the first time in this period. Judging by the crudity of the chipped flint arrowheads, these people were poor archers and preferred the spear and spearthrower in hunting and fighting. Pipes, like most artifacts except weapon heads, are rare. The "elbow" or L-shaped pipe is generally representative of the culture.

The six recognized Final Woodland subcultures with their diagnostic (though not very significant) traits are (1) Effigy Mound named for its distinguishing characteristic; (2) Tampico with pottery decorated with designs formed by cord-impressions, in northern Illinois; (3) Stone Vault with stone mounds containing walled tomb chambers; (4) Jersey Bluff with its unique "handled" tobacco pipes, in the west; (5) Raymond, best characterized by the generalized Woodland nature of its artifacts; and (6) Lewis with incised spiral designs on pottery, in southern Illinois.

A SECOND PLANT-RAISING CIVILIZATION—THE MIDDLE MISSISSIPPIANS (1000-1500 A.D.)

The Middle Mississippi culture seems to have arisen, as previously suggested, in the area where several important highways of aboriginal travel converged—the region surrounding the Ohio and Mississippi rivers from the mouth of the Wabash to the mouth of the Illinois. Whether or not its development was stimulated by the contracts of Muskhogeans and Algonkians or whether it was due to interplay between the cultures of the Final Woodland petty tribes is unknown.

Two slightly differing subcultures of the Middle phase appeared in the state. One, known archaeologically as the Cumberland (Tennessee-Cumberland), may have embraced at one time all the southern Illinois counties between the mouths of the Kaskaskia and the Wabash. [The Angel Site near Evansville, Indiana, may belong to the Cumberland subculture.] The other subculture, which may be termed Cahokia, flourished in counties bordering on the Mississippi from Union County to Wisconsin. As the two periods show few significant cultural differences, they will, except as noted hereafter, be treated as a single unit.

The bow and arrow invented in the Final Woodland phase, was developed early in the Middle Mississippi period into an effective weapon although spear and perhaps spearthrower continued in use. The chunkey game was probably played as a part of a religious ceremony though it may quite possibly have served as a popular pastime as well.

Pottery was slow at first to change from its more obvious Woodland characteristics but new shapes foreshadowing most of those of the fully developed (Old Village) cultural phase practically replaced the conical-based elongated pot early in the period. Cord-roughening and grit-tempering disappeared in the classic Cahokia period, and a fine polished blackware and a painted pottery were added to the smooth utilitarian ware. An excellent "dull gray" ware with smooth gray to brown surfaces was of more common occurrence. It appears to differ from the fine ware only in its partially oxidized surfaces probably due to poorly controlled firing methods.[14]

Fig. 23. The chunkey game in foreground. Man hunting with bow and arrow in background. Middle Mississippi period. (J.C.)

There were probably two or more social classes among the Middle phase people as there were among Hopewellians, Natchez and Polynesians.[15] The fine polished black and painted wares may have been marks of distinction between the highest and lower classes since it is much less common. In Hopewellian times, it is probable that both the fine ware and the specialized forms (which were usually of the highest quality) were reserved for the highest caste. In the Mississippi period, the shallow bowl, the cup or beaker, and the plate of dull gray ware seem to have been widespread in the village and may indicate a general improvement of living conditions among the lower social classes since Hopewellian times.

Fig. 24. Pottery shapes, Middle Mississippi period. A, "bean pot"; B, angular-shouldered pot or olla; C, common pot or olla; D, shallow bowl; E, water bottle; F, effigy bowl; G, plate.

Advances in the economy were obviously present in the fully developed Middle phase. The Union County flint "mines" and workshops were intensively worked. Trade with the Lake Superior, lower Atlantic and Gulf Coast regions was resumed. Chief imports of raw materials were copper and marine shells, Busycon, Marginella, Oliva and Olivella. Art, while possibly as highly developed as Hopewellian, resulted in a far smaller number of art objects in fewer durable media. Intaglio rock carvings (chiefly in southern Illinois) of geometric designs, human hands, ceremonial paraphernalia, animal outlines, and, in a few instances, painted hollowed-out animal silhouettes can probably be ascribed to this period on the basis of the symbols employed. Dwellings or cabins were relatively substantial structures and the extent of village remains indicate a large general population as compared to earlier times in the state. Trade and art suggest leisure and wealth or surplus available for exchange or to support officials and others in non-food productive pursuits. This prosperity was possibly due to newly discovered methods of intensive cultivation of maize and possibly to a greater diversity of crops than ever before.

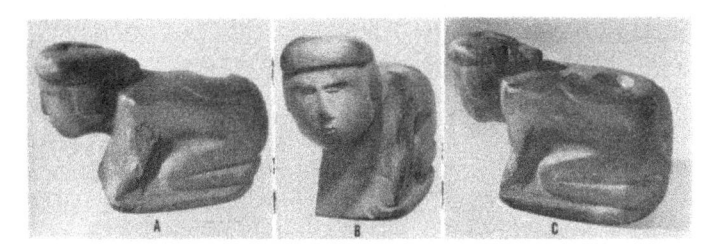

Fig. 25. Carved stone pipe (fragmentary) from Kingston Lake Site (Cahokia subculture, Middle Mississippi period). Owned by Donald Wray. Right-hand figure shows the pipe reconstructed.

Territorially the tribe probably consisted of a number of villages and the surrounding country. Each tribe may have had a chief village or capital that was also a religious center with tribal (public) buildings and a temple. Archaeological and historical evidence shows that these buildings, presumably temples and the dwellings of tribal chiefs and the high priests, were erected on the flat tops of rectangular earthen mounds or pyramids, which were grouped around a plaza of ceremonial square. Here the tribe gathered for religious and political ceremonies and for important funerals.

Intertribal negotiations and chunkey games were probably also staged on or near the plaza.

Pipes, either of stone or pottery, were generally of the "equal-armed" type (where stem length is about equal to bowl height). In numerous instances, a short projection resembling the stem in shape but shorter, extends beyond the bowl away from the smoker. Massive effigy pipes of stone were widespread but not numerous. Some were excellently carved. From their construction, it is obvious that they were made to be smoked through a reed or hollow wooden stem called in later times the calumet. These together probably constituted a form of ceremonial pipe that served as a safe conduct between tribes, as a bond and signature at peace- and treaty-making ceremonies, and to present tobacco smoke as incense to the gods in religious rituals.

Priests and possibly tribal chiefs were interred in the flat tops of mounds (e.g. the Powell Mound) near temple or cabin. Generally, however, the dead were buried in cemeteries. In some instances, bodies were laid on the surface above a "full" cemetery and covered with earth brought from outside. Continuing this practice eventually produced a mound (e.g. Dickson Mound near Lewistown). Possibly the burial mounds at Cahokia were reserved for the socially prominent while the lower classes were interred in the cemeteries nearby. The dead, especially important personages were attired in their finest apparel, insignia and personal ornaments. Beside them in the grave were placed their weapons, favorite chunkey stones, food and water in pottery vessels with shell spoons or a dipper.

Fig. 26. Interior view of Dickson Mound (in Dickson Mounds State Park near Lewistown, Illinois), showing pottery and other artifacts as originally placed with the dead. Cahokia subculture, Middle Mississippi phase.

Chief villages were large religious centers often protected by an encircling palisade or clay wall reinforced with vertical posts or logs. Remains of defensive walls can still be readily traced by a trained eye at the Kincaid (Massac County) and Lynn (Union County) villages. Exploration of the Aztalan village (Wisconsin) yielded remains of a reinforced clay wall surmounted at regular intervals with towers of like construction. The Cahokia village seems to have been without fortifications.

Fig. 27. Reconstruction of Kincaid Village (Cumberland subculture, Middle Mississippi period) near Metropolis, Illinois. (Diorama by Arthur Sieving.)

Smaller villages occasionally had one or two small flat-topped mounds which doubtless served as bases for the cabins of the Village Chief and possibly War Chief. Other Middle phase villages had no mounds or fortifications.

Cabins were of three or more types. In Illinois, two kinds had rectangular floor outlines and may have developed from the earlier Baumer square dwelling and the Lewis house. One of these types prevalent at Kincaid, as determined from charred remains, had a thatched gable roof supported on four corner posts with their lower ends sunk in the ground. Walls were made of clay daubed on a latticework of cane (with foliage) interlacing vertical wall posts, the interior covered with split cane mats. The rafters, corner and wall posts, and wall plates were of poles or small logs lashed together and held in place by braided ropes. Floors do not appear to have been depressed below surrounding ground level. A larger more substantial structure, presumably a temple, on a Kincaid mound (Mx°9) had thick walls of clay mixed with grass, but otherwise resembled the dwelling just described. The clay floor and wall surfaces were smooth. Fire basins of puddled clay within the building may have been the remains of altars.

Cabins in Fulton County (Fout's Village) and at Cahokia were rectangular in floor plan but wall posts were probably bent over to be joined with corresponding opposite members to form an arched or vaulted roof, the precursor perhaps of the "barrel-shaped" Illini cabins reported by French explorers. Floors were sunk somewhat below the ground level. Remains of cabins with circular floors occur also at Cahokia and in Fulton County.

Fig. 28. Petroglyphs from southern Illinois sites probably made by Middle Mississippian peoples. All figures are hollowed out or *intaglio*. (Photographs by Irvin Peithmann.)

Back wall of rock shelter near Gorham, Illinois.

Figure of buffalo calf painted yellow over entire depressed area. The outlines were chalked in for the purpose of photographing.

Walls and wall posts of the Fulton County cabins appear in some instances to be formed of bundles of small branches or cane set in trenches possibly a foot deep. There is no evidence of the wattle-and-daub structure. Walls may have been covered with mats, or with rectangles of bark. Roofs were probably thatched.

Possibly the Cahokia subculture peoples constituted a single tribe, a small nation, or a confederation of tribes. At its most powerful period, the Cahokia settlement was perhaps the capital and religious center. The region south of a line joining the mouths of the Kaskaskia and Wabash rivers at one time probably belonged to another tribe or subtribe whose chief village was the Kincaid community in Pope and Massac counties and who, linguistically and culturally, were closely related to peoples in Tennessee and Kentucky and at the Angel site in Indiana.

Archaeologically speaking, the Middle Mississippi contrasts sharply with the Hopewellian culture. Certain artifacts are readily distinguishable and easily identified with the craftsman's cultures. Actually the Mississippians differ from the Hopewellians chiefly in having substantial cabins, athletic games and the bow and arrow.

Remains of Hopewellian dwellings are rare, but the three or four found up to now are characterized by round or oval floor plans outlined with post holes of three to four inches in diameter. These seem to indicate hemispherical wigwams. No further evidence of wall or roof structure has been recovered. The rarity of these dwellings certainly suggests a less permanent dwelling than the Mississippi cabin. However, it will be remembered that some peoples pattern their tombs upon their dwellings. The upper caste Hopewellians built rectangular burial chambers which were walled up with logs laid one on another and roofed over with half-logs or bark. Similar log house surface structures would seldom leave discernible remains on decay. It is possible, though by no means certain, that the Hopewellians of highest caste, and perhaps of the other castes, built log cabins for dwellings.

The evidence for playing of athletic games in Hopewellian is very late and scanty. The only tangible indication are the rings, "pulleys" and a stone discoidal found with a skeleton in the Rutherford Mound. (See M. L. Fowler, *The Rutherford Mound*, Scientific Papers Series, Vol. VII, No. 1, Springfield, Ill. 1957, pp. 31-33). The rings of pottery and of cannel coal (or jet) seem too fragile for actual playing pieces and may rather be trophies or prizes, replicas of similar pieces made of wood. Such wooden pieces may have been used in games throughout middle and late Hopewellian times.

Fig. 29. (Photographs by Irvin Peithmann.)

View of a stream-side flint mine and workshop (in field alongside) near Cobden, Illinois.

Close-up showing spherical or "ball-flint" nodules from stream banks similar to those worked up by Middle Mississippians and others in adjacent workshop.

The bow and arrow, at least, seems to be a decided improvement over the spear. It constituted a repeating weapon. Ammunition could be carried in the belt or on the back in a quiver without unduly hampering the bowman. On the other hand, it was useless in hand-to-hand fighting and a spear or dagger was needed to supplement it. Moreover, the spear with a thrower was a more accurate weapon than the bow, unless the arrows were carefully made and balanced. The bow never seems to have wholly replaced the spear which continued to be a favorite weapon down into the European contact period.

The improvements that distinguish the Mississippians above the Hopewellians may be more apparent than real in the first two instances and, in the third, may represent a significant rather than a fundamental advance. Looking at the two periods from the broader cultural viewpoint, they appear to have many cultural features in common. The Middle Mississippians probably added new food and fibre plants to those of earlier periods, and perhaps increased production by improved, more intensive methods of cultivation. Their staple crops like those of the Hopewellians were corn, beans and tobacco.

The technologies or methods of making the necessary tools in the two cultures varied but little. Art was revived or rather redeveloped in the Mississippian period but fewer media are employed. In artistic skill, imagination and productiveness perhaps the Hopewellians had an edge on the later people.

Trade and travel, though resumed to distant sections of the continent, does not appear so widespread or general as in the Hopewellian period. A formalized religion with colorful ceremonies seems to have revitalized the life of the people but possibly no more effectively than in the earlier period.

There was no significant improvement in labor, power or transportation; all were still accomplished wholly by human effort without the aid of draft animals. Traveling by boat was known and probably used by both cultures.

Comparing the two peoples with other plant growers having no domestic food-draft animals, it seems apparent that each had an effective political organization, a formalized vital religion with true priests (not "self-appointed" shamans) and a system of moral values and tenets that "church" and "state" were organized to maintain. All in all, from the broader cultural standpoint, they were amazingly alike.

UNDER-DEVELOPED NEIGHBORS—THE UPPER MISSISSIPPIANS (1100?-1600 A.D.)

Less advanced Mississippi tribes with customs showing some admixture of Woodland cultural elements living contemporaneously in Missouri, Iowa, Wisconsin, Indiana and Ohio, encircled the Middle phase peoples on the east, north and west. Known generally now as the Upper phase peoples their sole representative in Illinois was the people of the Langford subculture, who dwelt around the southern end of Lake Michigan as well as in adjacent parts of Indiana and Michigan. The type station is the Fisher Village and Mounds near Joliet which were ably investigated by Mr. George Langford, Sr. some years ago.[16]

They built no flat-topped pyramids and left little, if any, evidence of their religious practices. Their art, as exhibited by pottery, personal ornaments or weapons was not of a high order. There is no evidence that they played the chunkey game. Some copper hatchets and ornaments were in use, but these appear to be of Middle Mississippi workmanship and may have been trade articles.

On the positive side, they buried their dead in dome-shaped earthen mounds, usually in the extended position, frequently with food (in clay pots with shell spoons), weapons (arrows and tomahawks or hafted celts), personal ornaments and various utilitarian implements. Dwellings had subsurface circular floors and were doubtless dome-shaped (hemispherical). The bow and arrow were in common use with arrowheads primarily of slender simple triangular shape, very rarely with side notches. Implements, weapons and ornaments were chiefly of chipped flint, ground or polished stone, river clam shells, bone and animal teeth. Copper was rarely employed.

Fig. 30. Characteristic pottery from the Langford subculture, Upper Mississippi phase, (Fisher Site near Channahon, Illinois). (Photograph by George Langford, Chicago Natural History Museum.)

Pots were generally of the globular or flattened globular shape (olla or jar), tempered with grit (early) and shell (later), and decorated with geometric designs in broad lines and dots, drawn ("trailed") or impressed on the shoulder region with a blunt tool (such as an antler tine). Lips of vessels were usually pressure-notched and surfaces cord-roughened. Loop handles on the jars were common.

Numerous examples of flat stone tablets associated with a number of short solid antler cylinders lead one to suspect that a game of chance of some sort was played and that gambling was probably indulged in.

Other than pottery and personal adornment, the only art practiced was the cutting of mussel shell into handled spoons and outlines of fish and other objects. Apparently there was no urge for fine workmanship.

It is highly probable that these Upper Mississippians were plant growers who hunted to secure their meat. The extent of village remains and the evidence of semi-permanent dwellings point to this type of economy even though no grain or seeds of any kind were found in the site. Shell hoes of the common type were used. The dog was the only domesticated animal.

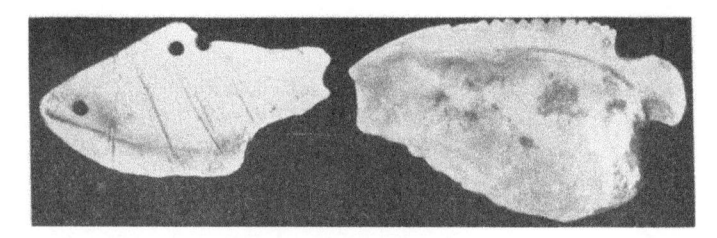

Fig. 31. Effigy fish and a decorated spoon (fragmentary) made of mussel shells. Langford subculture, Upper Mississippi phase (Fisher site). (Photograph by George Langford, Chicago Natural History Museum.)

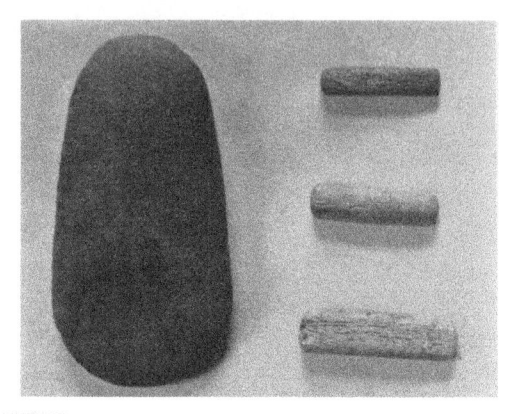

Fig. 32. Stone tablet and gaming pieces from the Langford subcultural period, Upper Mississippi phase (Fisher site). (Photograph by George Langford, Chicago Natural History Museum.)

Apparently most of their needs were supplied by their own efforts and from local sources. There is no evidence of any trade, except possibly of a very limited kind with near neighbors to the west.

The evidence for the residence around the southern lake shores is based chiefly on the occurrence of the Fisher pottery type. This area after 1760 was occupied by the Miami tribe who may possibly have been the builders of the Fisher Mounds.

THE ILLINOIS OR ILLINI[17] (1550?-1833 A.D.)

The Illinois or Illini Indians are, so far as is now known, the next group to occupy the state following the Middle Mississippians. At the time of Marquette and Jolliet's voyage in 1673, six tribes comprised the Illinois Confederacy, Kaskaskia, Cahokia, Michigamea, Peoria, Moingwena, and Tamaroa[18]. The tribes spoke the same or mutually intelligible dialects of the Algonkian language.

Some time before 1650, possibly a century or more, the Illinois Confederacy seems to have been a powerful nation but in the latter half of the 17th century this was a tradition rather than fact. The Confederacy appears to have engaged in no united action after 1650.

The Illini at that time were in the plant-raising stage of culture and possessed only the dog as a domesticated animal. Like many other plant-raisers, the families deserted the village for the hunt after the corn was hilled and again after the harvest.

Dress

Men went naked in summer except for mocassins. At times a breech cloth was worn; in winter buffalo skin robes were added and belts, leg bands and leggings on occasion.

Women when working apparently wore only a girdle (breech cloth), at other times a wrap-around skirt of skin with a belt passing over one shoulder and under the opposite arm. The skirt dates back to Hopewellian times and was used during the Mississippi period in Indiana and probably in Illinois. The bosom was covered with a deerskin wrap. Hair was worn long and fastened behind the head.

Economy

Labor was divided between the men and the women (and children). Men did the hunting, fighting and made the weapons. The women (and children) did the other work—the housework, planting and harvesting the crops, dressing deer and buffalo skins, making twine from bast, weaving cloth and, on the hunt, carrying the house parts and setting up the camp.

Buffalo meat was preserved by drying and smoking it over a fire in the hunting camp. Vegetable foods, corn, beans and squash were dried or parched and buried in containers or in lined pits in the ground and covered over. Watermelons, muskmelons (?), gourds and tobacco were also grown. Wild strawberries, paw paws, pecans, lotus roots, wild tubers, grapes and plums formed part of their diet.

The winter buffalo hunt usually took place a long way from the village. The hunting units each consisted of several families under a rigid police system and regulation to prevent the herd from being stampeded by an over-eager family before all were amply provided with meat. Violations of hunting regulations were punished by destruction of the offender's property to which no resistance was ever attempted. The group surrounded the herd, at times encircling it with fires made at intervals near which the hunters stood and killed the stampeding animals. At times as many as 120 buffalo were killed in a day. The women cut out the tongues, skinned the animals, and, peeling off the sides of meat, dried and smoked them on wooden grates over a slow fire. The smoked sides were carried back to the village on the back, or when practicable in dugout boats. Carcasses and bones were left on the hunting grounds. Other animals were stalked by one or two hunters. Dog meat was considered a great delicacy.

Fish were caught in nets, by hook and line, speared or shot with bow and arrow. They were dried for preservation. Maple trees were tapped late in the winter, the sap caught in bark containers and made into a maple drink or reduced by boiling to syrup and sugar. Corn was ground into meal and baked into bread, or prepared as hominy.

Vessels and utensils were made of wood or clay, ladles from a section of the buffalo skull. Fire was produced by the hand drill in the usual manner.

The cabin type seems to have varied at different periods or in different tribes. In early times, cabins had rectangular floors and vaulted (barrel-shaped) roofs. They were roofed and floored with "double-mats" of flat rushes and were impervious to wind or rain. Occasionally they were erected on low mounds (two feet high) to keep the floors dry. Large cabins of the vaulted type had four fires, with one or two families at a fire.

Bark-covered hemispherical huts or wigwams may have been used on hunting trips. They were apparently common in some villages in 1723.

Overland travel was on foot. On streams the dugout boat was propelled by pole and possibly by paddle. Large boats were 40 to 50 feet long, capable of carrying 40 to 50 men. While dugouts were admirably suited for travel and trade between the Illini tribes along the Illinois and Mississippi rivers, they were, on account of their weight and unwieldiness in portaging, generally useless in raids against enemies.

Fig. 33. Native Illini artifacts. A, Indian-made gun flint; B, C, D, chipped flint arrowheads; E, flint scraper; F, grooved abrader of sandstone; G, expanded base drill (grip only, point broken off); H, I, polished stone pendants. From Illini village site near mouth of Kaskaskia River, Randolph County.

Marriage Customs and the Family

An Illini man, desiring to get married, sent presents to the girl's parents. If the suitor was acceptable, the parents kept the gift and took the bride to the man's hut the following evening. Apparently there was no wedding ceremony.

Women had somewhat lower social status than their husbands. Wives did not eat with their husbands. A man was permitted two or more wives and often married two sisters. Children were well-treated. Infants were bound to a cradle board that the mother carried around. The cradle was pointed at the lower end and was stuck in the ground when the woman wanted to rest. Divorce was accomplished by a simple agreement to separate.

Political Organization

The explorers and writers to whom we are indebted for our knowledge of Illini social and religious organization were, unfortunately, casual and untrained observers who, on the whole, held the Indian and his customs in contempt. Important activities were often dismissed with meaningless generalizations, or omitted entirely, as if generally known. Consequently great gaps are left in the information that has come down to us.

From the various accounts, the impression is given that the Illini tribes (and possibly before the 17th century, the Confederacy) had a political government (rather than *family social control*) with formally appointed officers or civil chiefs. The Confederacy had one or more coats-of-arms ("totems") that may have been recognized abroad as symbolic of the Illini (as was customary among the Natchez and other southeastern Indians). It had a Grand Chief, chosen in some manner not now known, from one of the constituent tribes. At one period "Prince Tamaroa" of the Tamaroas held the post, later Chief Ducoigne of the Kaskaskias. Whether or not the Confederacy acted as a nation after 1600 is doubtful. Each tribe had its own head chief and coat-of-arms, and the French appear to have treated directly with the tribal heads in matters of importance. Judging from other Indian Confederations, the individual tribe had probably retained its full powers, and concerted action by the Confederacy was possible only by unanimous consent.

Like most peoples in the simple plant-raising status, the tribe dealt as a state with other similar units in intertribal affairs. These included alliances and treaties of peace. Ambassadors or tribal representatives were sent from Illini tribes to their neighbors. On such occasions, the calumet was carried and served as a safe conduct.[19] Tribal representatives met approaching strangers (and presumably the ambassadors of another tribe), raising the highly adorned calumet (and pipe) toward the sun as they advanced. Smoking the calumet—by the contracting tribal agents at the conclusion of an agreement—corresponded to our signatures and seals at the end of a written treaty.

Each village probably had a chief, whose power (it was sometimes reported) was little. However, the chiefs wore, as badges of office, red scarfs woven of bear and buffalo hair. Their faces were painted red. The village men (or possibly the important men) met before the village chief's cabin or in a large hut built especially for gatherings to deliberate on political or religious matters. The entire village often seems to have been in audience.

If there were social classes among the Illini, no mention is made of it in early reports. Men acquired prestige mainly through skillful hunting or success in fighting. The leader in a raid had to recompense the families of any followers killed in the fighting.

With so little description of the village and tribal assemblies and the chiefs in deliberation and judgment, it is difficult to determine the exact status of political organization of the tribe and its officers. It may well be that the powers of the chiefs immediately after European contact were small, and that in order to deal with the agency of a European state, the Illini found it necessary (as did the Delaware tribes) to grant greater authority and responsibility to their political leaders. It is probably also true that the chiefs would, under pressure from the whites, be reluctant to take responsibility for an unpopular concession and would declare that only the tribal council or assemblage could confirm the agreement under consideration. In any case, the Illini were on the threshold of true political control if they had not actually adopted it.

Raids

The tribe in historic times seems to have been the war-making group. Raiding parties tried to sneak undetected into enemy country and conceal themselves. From their hiding place, they fell suddenly on small unsuspecting enemy bodies, scalping men, killing women and children, and slipping away again with a few prisoners if practicable. Back in the village, captive warriors were bound to a frame of green wood, suspended over a slow fire, and tortured until death released them. Warriors hung the scalps taken upon their cabins as evidence of their prowess. The Illini claimed not to have tortured or burned captives until their men had been taken and so treated by Iroquois raiding parties. On the war path warriors carried bundles containing objects sacred to their guardian spirits and invoked them frequently to obtain victory.

Bows and arrows in quivers, hatchets or tomahawks, clubs, and "arrowproof" shields consisting of several layers of buffalo hide were carried on raids. The bow and arrow was considered superior to the gun because it could "fire" more rapidly.

Trade

Earlier in the European period, the Illini furnished Canadians with skins of beaver, raccoon, deer, bear and buffalo, but in 1776 the French (in Illinois) compelled them "to devote themselves to producing oil, tallow and meat which they traded with them." (Deliette Memoir. See Pease in Bibliography under ILLINI.) The Indians traded for porcupine quills with more northern neighbors. After the European came, Illini trade was probably overwhelmingly with the whites, exchanging native products of the forest for coveted guns, iron knives, hatchets, brass kettles, cloth, glass beads and alcoholic liquors.

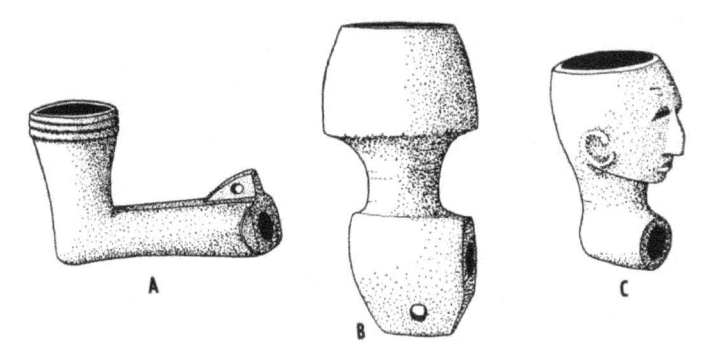

Fig. 34. A, B, common forms of Illini pipes (restored) of red Minnesota pipestone, Illinois State Museum collections: A, "Siouan"; B, Micmac; C, stone effigy-head type, (A. J. Throop collection). All from village near mouth of Kaskaskia River, Randolph County. (B.B.)

Religion

The religion of the early historic Illini was apparently a complex one. The sun was evidently a powerful deity from whom the calumet pipe had perhaps been supposedly received. A special calumet, apparently sacred to the sun, was revered as a palladium (like the Hebraic Ark of the Covenant) on which rested the safety of the nation. A special official had responsibility for its safe keeping. The smoke of the pipe was offered to the sun whenever the Illini prayed for rain, fine weather, or some other aid. Whether the Grand Manitou (Great Spirit), whom the French thought was the Supreme God of the Illini, was identical with the sun is not known though it seems probable.

In addition to the above gods, the Illini believed in numerous spirits and in reincarnation. A young man sought to secure a spirit as his superhuman helper or guardian for life. He fasted and prayed to the spirit to come to him in a vision. If successful (as he usually was), the spirit appeared to him in a dream and gave him instructions for a ritual by which he kept in contact with his protector. The objects needed for the ritual he collected on awakening and preserved them thereafter in a roll of painted matting. When calling upon his spirit protector, the bundle was opened and the rite performed, chiefly prayers and smoke offerings from a pipe blown toward the bundle.

It seems probable that there were true priests who were appointed by regular procedure and who received their power by virtue of their installation into office. The priests, we are told, painted themselves all over with clay on which designs were drawn. Their faces were painted with red, white, blue, yellow, green and black colors. The "high priest" wore a bonnet or crown of feathers and a pair of horns, possibly young deer or buffalo.

Medicine men also seem to have existed, persons who sought power from spirits to use in behalf of others for private gain or a livelihood. Possibly they were interested on the side in black magic or witchcraft, an anti-social activity.

Dancing, probably singing, and supplication, together with the inevitable smoke offerings from a ceremonial pipe doubtless formed a large part of public worship for which the whole community assembled. Details of the Illini ceremonies and their meanings are not known.

The French priests severely denounced native religious customs and "juggleries" of the Illini. The Peoria chiefs and priests resented this and resisted Christian attempts to convert the tribe (1693).

Funeral and burial customs seem to have been generally similar to those of other plant-raising peoples. All dead were treated with respect, decked in their best apparel, painted in preparation for burial. A dance was performed in honor of the deceased. A skin stretched over a large pot formed a drum which was beaten with a single stick as accompaniment for the dance. The participants were rewarded with presents at the conclusion of the dance. The gifts to be distributed were displayed in full view of the dancers and the duration of the dance was determined by their relative richness. An important personage was given special consideration and the whole community probably attended the funeral. Corn and a pot to boil it in were placed beside the dead. Friends standing around the grave threw into it bracelets, pendants and "pieces of earthenware" (pots?). The graves of chiefs were marked by a painted wooden post taller than the markers for ordinary people. Illini chiefs and persons of distinction as a signal honor were placed in tree-tops in a coffin made of bark. The tribe danced and sang for twenty-four hours during the funeral of a distinguished man.

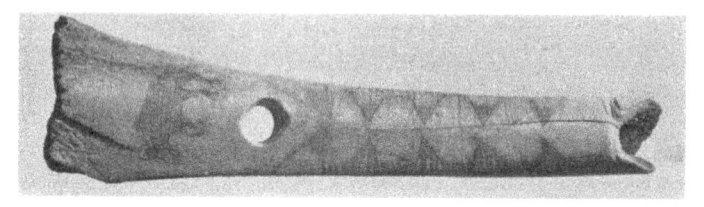

Fig. 35. Illini arrowshaft "wrench" or straightener of bison (?) rib engraved with figure of bison and cross-hatched triangles from Illinois village near mouth of Kaskaskia River, Randolph County.

Art

Men tattooed their "whole bodies." They painted themselves in solid colors and with designs in red, black, yellow, blue, and other colors. The body was adorned with native jewelry, the nose and ears were pierced for ornaments, and feathers of many colors were worn attached to the scalp lock. Moccasins were decorated with porcupine quill embroidery. Men clipped or shaved most of the head, leaving the scalp lock and four other tufts of long hair, two on each side, one in front of and behind each ear. After European trade goods were available, glass beads and cloth were obtainable in considerable quantities and largely replaced native dress materials and ornaments.

The Illini played lacrosse, an athletic game. The straw-and-bean game was a game of chance in which the players each took a number of straws from a bundle. The straws in each hand were discarded by sixes, the number left determining the winner of the round. Beans were used as counters. The Illini made wagers as to the outcome, even putting up their sisters as stakes in the game.

Fig. 36. Shapes of Illini pots (Middle Mississippi ware) reconstructed from sherds found in association with other native and European objects on the Illini village site near mouth of Kaskaskia River, Randolph County. (B.B.)

Archaeology of the Illini

Two village sites of the Illini have been investigated by the Illinois State Museum, one near Utica, LaSalle County (jointly with the University of Chicago) and one in Randolph County near the mouth of the Kaskaskia River. This last site was occupied for over a century by descendants of the Kaskaskias and other Illini tribes. Except for a small area where Archaic artifacts are found, it is a "pure" site.

The Illini tools, weapons and ornaments of native make were the usual chipped flint triangular arrowheads, simple flint drills and scrapers, rough stone hammers and abrading stones, small ground stone pendants, polished stone "Micmac" or "keel-based" pipe bowls (many of catlinite), the long-stemmed L-shaped catlinite pipes (sometimes called "Siouan"), and cut and engraved bone ornaments. An arrowshaft straightener carries an etching of a buffalo cow. Pottery is rare, but the pieces found in association with European trade goods are characteristically Middle Mississippian.

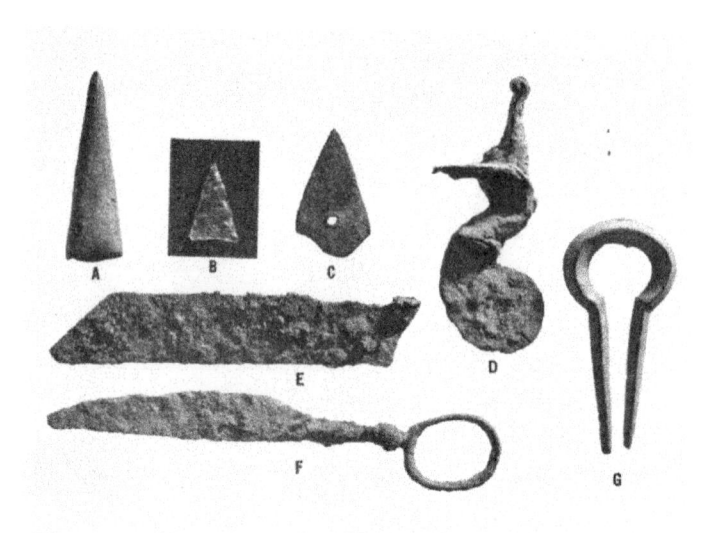

Fig. 37. European trade goods and artifacts made from European materials. All from Illini village near mouth of Kaskaskia River, Randolph County. A, conical arrowhead of sheet copper; B, chipped glass arrowhead; C, brass arrowhead; D, hammer of flintlock gun; E, iron blade of clasp knife; F, an iron scissor-blade; G, part of a jew's-harp.

The Illini made artifacts from fragments of European materials, iron spear- and arrowheads, brass and chipped glass arrowheads, brass pendants, and beads of broken porcelain.

European trade materials far exceed in number the native products. Usually they are fragmentary (except for colored glass beads of many kinds): parts of copper and brass kettles, iron handles, gun hammers and other parts, lead balls and the molds for making them, molds for casting crosses and ornaments, iron spoons, kitchen and clasp knife blades of iron, "Dutch" white pottery pipes, scissors, jew's-harps, bottles for wine and olive oil, brass buttons and finger rings.

The Illini seem to have cast lead into musket balls and chipped gun flints into shape but beyond that made no attempt to learn machine-age technologies. For firearms, gunpowder, iron knives and hatchets they were wholly dependent on the white invaders, a great disadvantage in event of hostilities and one that eventually cost them ownership of their ancient homelands.

THE INDIANS LEAVE ILLINOIS

For historic tribes of the state other than the Illini little is known of their archaeology. Culturally it is almost a certainty that all were, soon after contact, largely disorganized due to partial economic dependence, European diseases and the alcohol trade, to diminishing game, loss of other resources, and to military pressures from white governments and contiguous Indian groups.

Only the broad outlines of the movements of the historic tribes that lived, hunted, or made forays in Illinois need to be noted here. The Iroquois, Winnebago and Chickasaw made no attempts to permanently occupy Illinois territory as a result of their raids.

The Illini came under French influence after 1673 and leaned heavily on their military support. At times the Illini warriors fought bravely alongside the French, but generally they had little stomach for fighting even in their own defense. They shifted their settlements frequently after the Iroquois attack of 1680 and later under repeated pressure by the Sauk, Fox, Kickapoo and Potawatomi, who invaded and occupied the northern part of Illini territory.

Due to their dwindling courage and lack of incentive, more perhaps than to their losses in enemy raids, the Illini tribes decreased rapidly in numbers and importance. When they were removed to the west of the Mississippi in 1832, the population of the once great Illini Confederacy totalled little more than one hundred persons.

Even before this, the Miami had been pushed out of Illinois due to inroads of the Kickapoo and Potawatomi. The Shawnee, too, probably abandoned their permanent settlements in southern Illinois early in the contact period though these lower counties may have still been considered their territory. Other groups did not settle or hunt there and the Shawnee did establish some villages there (e.g. Shawneetown) briefly in the eighteenth century. Bands of Shawnee continued to hunt in this region until 1828 or later.

The Sauk, Fox, Kickapoo and Potawatomi did not long enjoy the territory they had wrested from the Illini and Miami. Immediately after the Black Hawk War in 1832, steps were taken to move all Indians from the state. By the Treaty of Chicago, the Indians gave up all their lands in Illinois, and in 1837 the last bands

(Potawatomi) crossed to the western bank of the Mississippi. No land is reserved today in this state for Indians. Its former resident tribes now live in reservations in Iowa, Oklahoma, Kansas, Nebraska and in the state of Coahuila in Mexico.

SUMMARY OF ILLINOIS PREHISTORY

The archaeology of Illinois in its present position seems to indicate that the state did not at any time form a distinct single culture or subculture but that it was rather the meeting place of many, due possibly to the rivers that enclose, lead to and intersect its territory. It was at one and the same time a part of one or more widespread patterns or phases and a patchwork of subcultures that extended into neighboring states. There was a tendency for the cultures of the northern four-fifths of the state (roughly north of a line joining East St. Louis with Evansville, Indiana) to be more like the adjacent regions, while those of the remaining counties were more closely related to those of Kentucky, Tennessee, southern Indiana and Missouri and rather readily distinguishable from those of their northern neighbors.

There are few instances when it appears probable that a part of the state was invaded by a people of a distinctly differing culture. The Paleo-Indian Big Game Hunters presumably found in Illinois virgin country without previous human occupants. The Baumerians probably entered Illinois from south of the Ohio and expelled or absorbed the conservative Terminal Archaics. Possibly Mortonians intruded into the Black Sand-Red Ocre culture of Illinois from the northwest. Less plausibly, the Stone Vault Grave people may have pushed their way into Adams County from the Gasconade River region of Missouri.

The emphasis in this paper has been placed perhaps on the change of cultures. To keep one from getting an erroneous impression of cultural stability, it should be said that, in the writer's opinion, a culture and subculture contained in greater or smaller areas change gradually through a process of invention here and there and through interchanges of improvements back and forth over a long time. When the change is sufficient to be noted as a "new" culture, the various cultural elements or features are apt to be widely distributed over much the same area. Thus, Baumer seems to have existed for a time alongside Terminal Archaic but finally spread through the southern counties; Hopewellian may have persisted in Calhoun County for a century or more after its collapse to the north and east; and the Final phase may have lingered on in remote portions of the state until Cahokia was past the height of its glory. In general, perhaps it could be said that the southern fifth and the remaining four-fifths of the state were out of step with each other most of the time.

As previously noted, some of the Paleo-Indian families, upon the retreat of the last glacier, settled in Illinois as they did in the neighboring states, adapted themselves to the changed surroundings, and in so doing developed the Archaic culture or way of life. This phase developed through a series of subcultures though not necessarily identical sequences in all the states or even within Illinois. In southern Illinois, Terminal Archaic seems to have persisted until about 2000 B.C. while in the north, it apparently had developed into Initial (early) Woodland a few centuries earlier. The Baumer subculture, probably arising from the Archaic of Tennessee, appears to have been carried by its bearers into southeastern Illinois along the Tennessee and Cumberland rivers. Although widespread in the Mississippi Valley, the Archaic population was thinly scattered.

In northern Illinois and in Wisconsin the Black Sand-Red Ochre culture seems to have developed from the native Terminal Archaic (and Old Copper) possibly around 2500 B.C. The Morton (Central Basin) people appear to have had their cultural roots outside the state and to have combined with the native groups (Black Sand-Red Ochre) they found in the northern counties. Average populational distribution was still low with the small settlements perhaps somewhat more numerous though no more populous than during Archaic times. The early Woodland peoples differed from their predecessors mainly in being pottery-makers. In southern Illinois only they practiced storage of acorns and hickory nuts extensively.

About 500 B.C. in northern Illinois the Morton people more or less contemporaneously with similarly advanced peoples in Iowa, Wisconsin, Indiana, Michigan and Ohio, passed into the Hopewellian civilization which was erected on the cultivation of maize, beans, squash and tobacco, and the technologies of the earlier Woodland period. In southern Illinois Baumer developed into the Crab Orchard culture whose people traded with the more northern Hopewellians, intermarried with them and finally adopted the Hopewellian way of life about 100 B.C.

A century or two later, Hopewellian in the north of Illinois began to deteriorate and eventually broke up into a number of small subcultures, obviously closely related but still distinguishable archaeologically. The same disintegration of Hopewellian took place in southern Illinois a few centuries later, and by 400 or 450 B.C. Hopewellian had disappeared from all Illinois except possibly in Calhoun County in the west, while south of the Ohio

River it still continued to spread and flourish in Mississippi and Louisiana for some centuries.

In Illinois a period of decadence set in for the next few centuries (possibly 250 to 1000 A.D.). The larger settlements or settlement clusters dwindled to mere hamlets, whose remains are scarcely distinguishable from the early Woodland artifacts except that the tobacco pipe is present. Though they must still have retained a tradition of plant-raising, they seem to have avoided it and reverted to a pure hunting-collecting economy. Even in southern Illinois the storage of food seems to have played an insignificant role. Nevertheless throughout this cultural recession, certain trends occur in all the six Final Woodland subcultures which foreshadow later developments in the Middle (Mississippi) Phase.

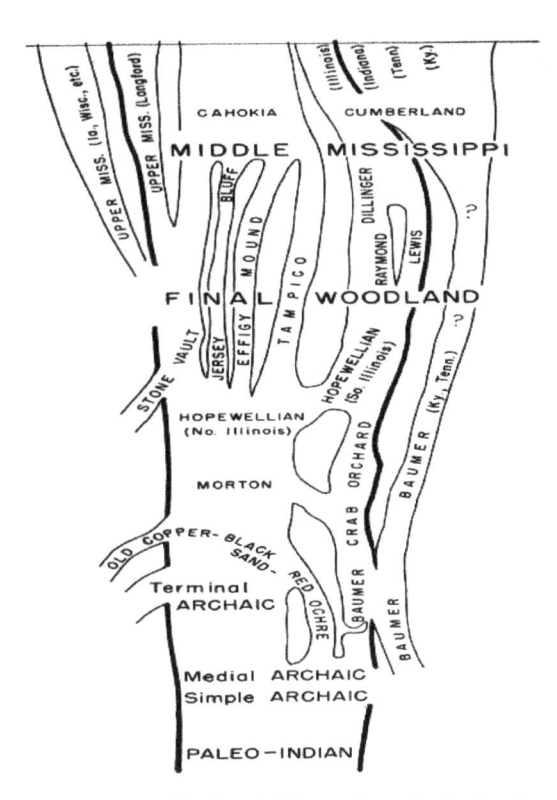

Fig. 38. The Stream of Culture. The archaeological cultures within Illinois are included within the two heavy lines, openings in which indicate cultural extensions beyond or intrusions into the state. Vertical positions indicate sequences in a general way. (Drawing by Jeanne McCarty.)

About 1000 A.D. or possibly a little earlier, the Final Woodland developed into an early Protomississippi (Protomiss) and, at last, (possibly 1000 to 1100 A.D.) into the full-blown Middle Phase civilization. The Cahokia subculture appears to be primarily, though not exclusively, Illinoisian while the Cumberland development in the southeast of the state was shared more generously with adjacent Indiana, Kentucky and Tennessee. Judging by the distribution of stone box (cist) graves, the Cumberland subculture seems to have expanded westward at the expense of the Cahokia peoples to envelope most of the southern counties from Monroe to White. (Another interpretation might be that the grave type of their eastern Cumberland neighbors was adopted by the Cahokians.) The Crable Village, possibly a late Cahokian settlement, yields artifacts suggesting cultural influences brought in from Iowa, Missouri and possibly Arkansas. It is probable that the culture came to an end in Illinois by 1500 or 1550. This fact coupled with the pottery evidence makes it highly probable (though possibly not conclusive) that the disorganized Illini Confederacy embraced the tribes whose members were the descendants of the people of the great Middle Phase civilization in Illinois.

More or less contemporaneous with the Middle Phase culture were the so-called Upper Phase peoples of Missouri, Iowa, Wisconsin, Michigan and Indiana. These were represented in Illinois by the Fisher peoples of the Langford subculture known chiefly from sites along the Illinois, Kankakee and Des Plaines rivers in northeastern Illinois and (chiefly on a pottery basis) in northwestern Indiana and southern Michigan.

Beset by enemies on the east, south, north and northwest, with their traditions of former greatness fading, the demoralized Illini tribes welcomed the protection of French soldiers. Their own resourcefulness, courage, pride, and confidence in themselves and their culture continued to deteriorate, their numbers to diminish under the softening influence of alcohol and the persistent assaults of the ruder more aggressive Winnebago, Sauk, Fox, Potawatomi and Kickapoo tribes invading Illinois from the north until they were reduced by 1833 to a mere handful of a hundred odd men, women and children. The demands on the part of citizens of the United States for Illinois lands was brought to a head by the scare of the Black Hawk War, and the Illini, their traditional Indian friends and enemies, were transferred to new territory west of the Mississippi. Thus ended the aboriginal occupation of Illinois that had endured for at least 10,000 years.

GLOSSARY

ADVANCED PHASE: The earliest pottery-making cultures of Woodland in southern Illinois. The peoples seem to have been storers of acorns and hickory nuts. It is sometimes called early Woodland.

AMERINDIAN: The American Indian of Mongolian racial stock so named to distinguish him from the Asiatic Indian who is of the white or Caucasian race.

ANTHROPOLOGY: The study of man and his cultural activities.

ARCHAEOLOGY: The division of anthropology that studies peoples of the past through the remains of their works that are found in the ground.

ARCHAIC (SUBCULTURE): An archaeological subdivision of the Lithic Pattern characterized by broad-bladed barbed spearheads, spearthrower weights and "bannerstones," small camps, and a hunting-collecting economy (without plant-raising or food-storage).

ARROWHEADS: Projectile points less than three inches long presumed to have been used to tip arrows.

ART: A form of human endeavor in which the individual or artist, with more or less skill, tries to produce an object or activity of such a nature that it is esthetically satisfying in some sense both to himself and to his group generally.

ARTIFACTS: Any object made by man, or a natural object modified by man, in order to satisfy a cultural need. (Only the names and uses of artifacts that are not self-explanatory appear in the glossary).

ATLATL: See SPEARTHROWER.

ASSEMBLAGE: In this paper assemblage refers to the selected significant artifact types of an archaeological unit. In a more general sense, it signifies the aggregate of artifacts found at a particular site, or in a deposit belonging to a single culture at the site.

AX: Refers in this paper to the grooved ground stone head resembling the modern steel ax in general form and presumably used for chopping in a somewhat similar manner.

AZTALAN: The site of a Middle Phase fortified village with mounds in Jefferson County, Wisconsin, in the Cahokia Subculture. It was investigated by the Milwaukee Public Museum. See S. A. Barrett in Bibliography.

BARB: A projection or shoulder near the base of the blade of a spear, dart or arrowhead that serves to retain it in a wound and to stimulate bleeding. One of a number of "backward" projections on a harpoon that serves a similar purpose.

BAST: The inner bark (phloem) of a tree.

BREECH CLOTH or CLOUT: An article of clothing consisting of a narrow band or fold of cloth or skin that passes around the waist and between the legs.

BURIAL MOUND: Any man-made hill or knoll erected primarily to enclose the dead.

CACHE: A deposit of a large number of artifacts in a grave or, in general, a number of artifacts found together in the earth.

CALUMET: See note, page 48.

CELT: An ungrooved stone or copper hatchet head.

CHIEF: An official selected and formally installed in office by some social process who exercises civil authority by virtue of office.

CHIPPING: See Flaking.

CHOPPER: Generally any tool used for chopping, hewing, or hacking. Specifically, a chipped flint tool roughly hatchet shaped. Some hand choppers have the edge of the blade paralleling the longer axis of the piece.

CHUNKEY STONE: A polished stone disk that was used as a bowl in various types of games.

CIVILIZATION: See note, page 26.

CLASSIC: The term used in this paper to designate the phase to which the Hopewellian Civilization of the Woodland pattern belongs.

CLOVIS POINT: A type of leaf-shaped spearhead with a longitudinal groove (channel or fluting) generally extending one fourth to one half the length of the piece from its base toward its tip.

CLUB: An adaptation of a stick for a weapon or a tool for hurling (throwing stick) or battering (war club). The war club is often weighted with a stone head for greater effectiveness. It differs from the tomahawk in that it has no cutting edge.

CONCHOIDAL FRACTURE: The property of flint and certain other stones when struck with a hammer of chipping away in flakes which leave concave or shell-like scars or hollows. By suitable control methods, tool and weapon heads of desired types can be produced.

CONOIDAL or CONICAL BASE: The characteristic pointed base of Woodland pots.

CRAB ORCHARD: A division of the Baumer subculture.

CULTURE: Culture as used in this paper has one of two meanings, each readily understood in its context. In a general sense, it means the significant beliefs, customary activities and social prohibitions peculiar to man (together with the man-made tools, weapons and other material objects that he finds or has found necessary) that modify, limit or enhance in some manner, most of his discernible natural activities due to his physical animal inheritance and organization. Culture in a specific sense refers to the significant cultural features of the group or period under consideration, the way of life. See FEATURE, CULTURAL.

CUMBERLAND: A subculture of the Middle (Mississippi) Phase that flourished in southern Illinois, western Kentucky and Tennessee, archaeologically known as Gordon-Fewkes or Tennessee-Cumberland.

DAGGER: A long sharp-pointed blade of flint (or a copper pin) presumably hafted with a wooden handle, used as a hunting knife or in hand-to-hand fighting.

DARTHEADS: Medium-sized weapon heads (2½ to 4 inches long) presumably used to tip lances or javelins.

DICKSON MOUND: A burial mound near Lewistown in Fulton County where some three hundred skeletons together with their grave offerings have been exposed to view. It is now a State Park and open to visitors.

DIGGING STICK: A conveniently-shaped stick used by primitive peoples in collecting tubers and roots and small animals, digging storage pits, and for preparing the soil for planting. Antler was sometimes shaped and presumably employed in like manner.

DIGGING TOOL: Any implement employed by primitive peoples in digging—a digging stick, a shell hoe, or a chipped flint hoe.

DOMESTICATION: The breeding and rearing of plants and animals under man's control and for his needs.

DRIFT (rarely drifter): A blunt tool of antler or bone presumably held in the hand and pressed against a flint to flake it, or one held against the flint piece and struck with a hammer for a like purpose.

DUGOUT: A boat made by hollowing out a log with fire and tools and shaping its exterior suitably for water travel.

ECONOMIC ASPECT: That division of primitive culture concerned primarily with securing and preparing food, shelter, clothing, and raw materials for tools, weapons and other material devices, and the technologies involved. This required considerable knowledge of natural resources, properties of materials, and lay of the land and permits freer direct creative intellectual effort than does any other aspect.

ECONOMY: The chief means of securing food and other basic physical requirements of man, as a hunting-collecting economy.

EFFIGY: Any artifact resembling in outline, in relief, or in the round some living organism or mythical being.

EFFIGY MOUND: A mound of earth in low relief shaped in outline form to resemble an animal or some geometric or other conventionalized form. They are often found in groups together with conical and elongated or linear mounds in Minnesota, Wisconsin, Iowa and Illinois.

EFFIGY POT: A pottery vessel made in the form of an animal, human being, or a part of one, or having conventionalized bird or animal head and tail projecting from opposite sides of rim or mouth (generally of shallow bowls), occurring most commonly in the Middle (Mississippi) Phase.

EXTENDED: As applied to burials, a skeleton lying at full length usually on its side or back.

FAMILY, EXTENDED: A man, his wife or wives, their descendants in the male or female line as custom dictates, and their families who consider themselves as a distinct social unit usually with an acknowledged leader or headman. The extended family usually lives in a local settlement or a limited territory.

FAMILY, SIMPLE: A man, his wife or wives and their unmarried children.

FAMILY-TYPE SOCIAL CONTROL: The manner of maintaining peace, order, and obedience to elders and to custom in tribes and local groups in the Self-Domestication Stage secured by early and strict indoctrination of the young in the family and through public opinion (social approval and disapproval) rather than by force and political agencies.

FEATHER CLOTH: Robes or blankets made by attaching overlapping feathers to the outer surface of a textile or netting to simulate a bird skin.

FEATURE, CULTURAL: Any type of cultural organization (or institution) within a tribe or independent cultural unit such as marriage, the family division of labor, social control, political governing agency, Sacred Tradition ("mythology"), etc.

FERTILITY RITES: The religious ceremonies performed in a primitive tribe for the purpose of insuring its welfare, the continuance of an abundant supply of food animals and other natural resources on which it depends, and possibly with expressions of gratitude for past benefits.

FESTIVALS: The term applied to the religious ceremonies of plant-raising peoples that relate to planting and the harvesting of crops.

FINAL PHASE: The decadent Woodland culture, archaeologically known as late Woodland, is characteristic of much of Illinois in the interval between the fall of Hopewellian and the rise of Mississippi.

FLAKER (DRIFT): A flint-working tool either used alone with simple pressure or as a punch struck by a stone hammer (indirect percussion).

FLAKING or CHIPPING: The method of working flint into tools and weapons by direct hammer blows, indirect percussion or by pressure with a flaker.

FLEXED: As applied to burials, a skeleton (generally lying on its side) with knees drawn up to or near chest, arms close to side or with hand(s) near head.

FLINT: In this paper, any stone that flakes with a conchoidal fracture that was so used by Amerindians to make chipped tools and weapons.

FOLSOM POINT: A flint spearhead having the faces of the blade hollowed out by chipping (channeling or fluting) except for a narrow strip paralleling each edge including the tip (see Figure 3, page 11).

FOOD-DRAFT ANIMALS: The large mammals (especially the ox) that were domesticated by man and besides providing him with a continuously available supply of meat, served as a beast of burden or to draw a wheeled vehicle, to drag the plough, and as a source of energy to turn the mill. Animals were not generally so used in North America.

FOOD-STORERS: Those peoples who by virtue of native ingenuity and some special natural resource in their region were enabled to store up sufficient food supplies to last them for several months.

FORMALIZED RELIGION: The forms of prayer, worship, devotion and ritual and the organization of priests, etc. by which plant-raising tribes carry on their assumed relationships with the world of the unknown agents of natural forces.

GORGET: (pronounced gor´-jet) A large flat artifact, possibly at times an insigne, of stone, shell, copper or bone worn on the chest.

GRAVE GOODS: The jewelry, insignia, weapons or implements of a dead tribesman together with offerings that may have been placed in his grave by friends or relatives, including vessels containing food and water. Also called beigaben, funeral offerings, grave furniture, etc.

GRINDING: The process by which a stone, bone, shell or metal artifact was shaped by rubbing with sand and water or against a piece of sandstone (abrader).

GRINDING STONE: A large flat or slightly hollowed stone on which seeds, berries, or nuts were crushed or ground by a smaller hand stone (muller or pestle).

GUARDIAN SPIRIT: Among primitive peoples, a being from the invisible spirit world who appeared to a person in a dream and was believed to serve the dreamer thereafter as his personal protector.

HAMLET: The name used in this paper for local settlements of Archaic and Initial Woodland sites. They probably had populations of less than one hundred persons.

HAMMERSTONE: A stone hammer. Any native or modified cobblestone used as a hammer.

HATCHET: A ground stone or copper celt head. Tomahawk or hafted hatchet.

HOUSEHOLD: A man, his wife, and children, married and unmarried together with slaves and others, if any, who customarily in their culture live under one shelter or roof.

INDIRECT PERCUSSION: The use of a punch with a hammer, especially in the chipping of stone.

INITIAL PHASE: The earliest pottery-making cultures of Woodland in northern Illinois, archaeologically known as early Woodland.

INITIATION RITES: Puberty rites. As used in this paper, the ceremonies by which a boy on "becoming of age" is admitted to adult membership in the tribe. Somewhat simpler rites are performed for girls also in some tribes.

INSIGNE: (Plural *insignia*) Any artifact worn by primitive people as a symbol of rank or class, birth (in a particular family), office, priesthood, or of individual prowess.

INSTITUTIONS: See Social Structure.

JEWELRY: Any object other than insignia, paint, or clothing worn by primitive man as personal adornment.

KINCAID COMMUNITY: The site of a Middle Phase village, mounds, fortifications and other cultural remains in Pope and Massac counties, Illinois, on the Ohio River a few miles above Paducah, Kentucky.

LAKE BAIKAL: A large inland lake in the south of Siberia. Pottery from the surrounding region resembles generalized Woodland ware, especially that of the Initial Phase.

LINEAGE: The social group (including dead persons) whose members are descended from some certain or mythical ancestor, either male or female as the custom prevails, and which considers itself a distinct social unit. (See also Extended Family.)

LITHIC: A term employed in this paper as embracing cultures roughly equivalent to those of the Self-Domestication Stage, but without pottery.

MANA: Superhuman power that primitive man believed to reside in certain inanimate objects, in certain persons at times and in spirits, that under suitable conditions could be transferred either wholly or in part to other objects or persons. Improperly handled it was a source of grave danger.

MIDDLE PHASE: The archaeological term for the highest development of the Mississippi pattern in the United States. In Illinois it is represented by the Cahokia and Cumberland subcultures.

MISSISSIPPI: The major archaeological pattern that succeeded the earlier Woodland in most of the United States east of the Rocky Mountains and High Plains and that was still in existence in some parts of this country as late as 1700 A.D. It is characterized by relatively intensive plant-raising, political government, walled villages, temples (or sacred groves) and a priesthood, semi- to permanent dwellings, pottery of varied shapes, with globular bodies and secondary features, the bow and arrow.

MODOC ROCK SHELTER: An ancient settlement of Archaic peoples in Randolph County, Illinois, dating from 8000 to 2100 B.C. See Bibliography under Deuel, and Fowler and Winters.

MOUND: Any rise or hill of earth and/or stone that resulted from some activity of man, such as refuse mound, shell mound, burial mound, temple mound, etc. See BURIAL, EFFIGY, TEMPLE.

MOUND BUILDERS: A term having little significance, meaning any group that erected mounds. In American archaeology it sometimes refers specifically to Hopewellians, to Mississippians or to both.

MYTHOLOGY: See SACRED TRADITION.

OBSIDIAN: Volcanic glass, a material imported by Hopewellians possibly from Wyoming. Rare in Illinois.

PALEO-INDIAN (See Clovis and Folsom): Hunters of big game who roamed over North America in glacial times.

PATTERN: The largest archaeological unit in the McKern Classification System.

PECKING: The process (other than chipping) by which a stone artifact was brought to general shape by breaking off small particles with a stone hammer.

PEOPLE: The term "people" as used in this paper does not refer to a physical type but simply to cultural groups unless specifically stated to the contrary.

PERIOD: Unless otherwise specifically stated, the word applies to a cultural level regardless of time and place.

PHASE: The major division of the pattern as used in the McKern Classification System.

PLANT-RAISING: The economy or cultural status of a cultural group who grew food (and fibre) plants but were without domesticated food-draft animals.

POLITICAL ORGANIZATION: A formalized social means of controlling the members of a nation or tribe and compelling compliance with established customs or laws with defined customary or lawful penalties for violations together with the machinery for determining equity, rights, or damages in non-criminal disputes through governmental agencies such as officers (chiefs) and official bodies (councils) regularly selected for these purposes.

POLISHING: A process by which the surface of a ground stone artifact was brought to a high degree of smoothness and gloss by rubbing with fine earth and water. It is readily distinguishable from polish due to wear in digging.

PRIEST: Any person selected in a regular and customary manner for religious office who by virtue of installation into that office and acceptance of the duties is (believed to be) invested with the power to communicate and intercede with members of the spirit world, a god or gods or in certain instances to act for them on behalf of his group.

PRIMITIVE PEOPLE: Refers to any people in the Self-Domestication Stage and to the simple plant-growers of the Farming Period.

PROTOCULTURAL: A stage presumed to have existed prior to man's discovery of the principle of conchoidal fracturing of flint, when he used native sticks and stones as tools, and sometimes by haphazard breaking of these secured new forms more suitable for his purposes.

PROTOMISS: An abbreviated form for Protomississippi, the earliest known subculture of the Middle (Mississippi) Phase in southwestern Illinois. Dillinger is the type site.

RELIGION: The set of beliefs (Sacred Tradition), rules (tabus), and activities (including rituals) that govern the life of a society with regard to those superhuman forces with which the individual feels himself surrounded and which neither he nor his group by themselves can control. Religious practice includes prayers or requests for the continuance of well-being and life's necessities, thanksgiving for past blessings, and a belief in the necessity of right conduct of the individuals in their daily living. In all known primitive religions, a belief in some form exists of spirit beings and/or gods with superhuman powers. See FORMALIZED RELIGION.

ROCK SHELTER: An overhanging rock ledge facing away from the prevailing wind that afforded protection to a primitive family from the elements and wild animals.

ROUGH STONE: This term refers to stone used as it occurs in nature with virtually no artificial modification other than that resulting from use such as a common hammerstone, an unworked abrader, or a grinding stone. The stone may have a relatively smooth surface due to natural causes.

SACRED TRADITION: The term used here to signify the embodiment of the significant (effective) beliefs and rules that governed the behavior and activities of a primitive tribe in matters relating to the unseen world of spirits (or gods) and unknown forces, which were handed down from generation to generation. It is usually included in the inept term "mythology" which may also contain tales and legends that serve for mere entertainment.

SELF-DOMESTICATION STAGE: The earliest stage of true human culture which began presumably with the discovery of controlled flint chipping and the invention of flint tool types. During this stage, man is enabled to secure a fairly constant food supply by hunting and collecting, keeps his young under parental care and control for several years and learns to accommodate himself more or less peaceably to his family and to fellow tribesmen during brief periods of religious and social gatherings.

SHAMAN: A person who by virtue of dreams or visions believes he can communicate with spirits, obtain from them superhuman powers for the benefit of his social group and tribe and who has demonstrated these abilities over a greater or longer time to the satisfaction of his fellows.

SHELLS, MARINE: Shells from the ocean or Gulf of Mexico, raw materials secured by traders or through exchange for other goods. The most common marine shells found in Illinois cultures are the *Cassis madagascarensis* (Hopewellian), the Busycon or Fulgar (Middle Mississippi and Hopewellian), *Marginella* (Initial Woodland, Hopewellian and Middle Mississippi), *Oliva* (Middle Mississippi), and *Olivella* (Hopewellian).

SOCIAL ASPECT: That division of primitive culture that is concerned preeminently with preserving and stabilizing fundamental customs, with the maintenance of peace and order within its primary social units, and to this end, in the organization, functioning and continuation of such units.

SOCIAL CONTROL: Any general social means by which a social or political group preserves peace and order within itself and group protection against outsiders (see Family-type and Political Agency).

SOCIAL STRUCTURE: The persisting system of significant relationships in a society that prevails without regard to the particular individuals involved.

SPEARHEADS: Projectile points 3 to 6 or 6½ inches long presumed to have been used to tip spears.

SPEARTHROWER (ATLATL): A short stick by which increased leverage is obtained in hurling a spear. It gives greater range and an accuracy comparable to the bow at shorter distances.

SPEARTHROWER WEIGHT: A weight secured to the spearthrower for controlling it and increasing the speed of the spear.

SPEAR, THRUSTING: A long spear that is fitted with a long, narrow head generally without barbs or shoulders, that can be easily withdrawn from a wound. It is primarily for use in the hand, not for throwing.

SPECIALIZATION (CRAFT): An occupation in which a man or household of a primitive community engages primarily to the considerable exclusion of the general economic pursuits or the remainder of his group. It should not be confused with the production of a highly skilled craftsman.

SPECIALIZATION (OF TOOLS): Applies to numerous variations in the forms derived from a general artifact type presumably to accomplish better and more easily certain special requirements of construction or manufacture.

STAGE (CULTURAL): One of the major periods into which cultures may be divided by virtue of its degree of development which depends primarily on the fundamental invention that ushered it in.

SPIRITUAL ASPECT: That division of primitive culture concerned primarily with tribal values, religion, recreation and the arts.

STATUS (CULTURAL): A subdivision of a stage. A substage.

STONE: Unless otherwise noted any kind of stone generally used by primitive peoples for pecking, grinding and polishing into weapons, tools, etc., for example, granite, greenstone, gneiss, shale, limestone, basalt.

STONE VAULT GRAVE: A type of burial mound consisting chiefly of flat stones enclosing a walled-up tomb chamber, the whole covered with earth. In Illinois known at present only from Adams County.

STONE VAULT SUBCULTURE: A division of Final Woodland Phase that is characterized by stone vault graves.

SUBCULTURE: Any archaeological grouping smaller than a phase.

SUBSTAGE or STATUS: A subdivision of a *Stage* that develops as the result of a significant invention, discovery of a special resource, or some other condition of the surroundings.

TECHNOLOGY: The processes by which any artifact is produced.

TEEPEE: A conical framework of poles covered with bark, skins, brush, mats, etc. used as a shelter or hut by primitive peoples.

TEMPERING: Foreign material such as sand, crushed limestone, plant fibers, crushed shell, etc. mixed with the clay in pottery-making to render the vessel less likely to crack in firing.

TEMPLE MOUND: A rectangular pyramid with a flat top on which a temple was built. Similar mounds were used for council and chief's houses among historic Mississippi peoples. Flat-topped pyramidal mounds are characteristic of the important Middle Mississippi sites in Illinois.

THERMAL MAXIMUM: A time interval (roughly between 5000 and 2000 B.C.) in which the climate was warmer and drier than at present.

TOMAHAWK: A hafted hatchet of stone or metal used in fighting.

TOTEM: An animal, plant or inanimate object that is regarded as the symbol of a social or political group.

TUMPLINE: A sling or pack strap that rests on the forehead, passes over the shoulders, and is used for carrying a load on the back.

TURKEY-TAIL: A large spearhead, broadly oval in the middle and double-pointed with notches near one end.

TYPE STATION(S): The site (or sites) that at present seem, to the author, to give the fullest view of life in a subculture, including as far as possible a village (or camp) and burial site.

WAR (ARCHAIC): The blood feud. In the Archaic period, this was the method of interfamily or intergroup retaliation for murder or other serious injury to one family or local group by a member of another. It was carried on by alternate sneak raids between the local settlements involved, with the object of killing one or more members of the group attacked, (destroying property), and escaping without loss.

WAR (PLANT-RAISERS): Hostilities between plant-raising tribes were pursued by sneak raids having for their objectives the surprise and attack of villages, the ambush of enemy parties, and the capture of prisoners. (Murder, black magic, and other crimes committed within the tribe were generally dealt with by socio-judicial custom).

WATTLE AND DAUB: A framework of posts, interlaced with branches and twigs and plastered over with clay for house and fortification walls common in Middle Phase and probably in other periods.

WIGWAM: As used here, a roughly hemispherical hut having a framework of poles set in the ground with their tops arched over and secured together, the whole covered over with leafy branches, skins, bark, mats or thatch.

WINDBREAK: A vertical or inclined framework of poles covered with branches and leaves, skins, bark, etc. erected by primitive peoples as a shelter against wind, sun, and storm.

WOODLAND: One of the major archaeological patterns of the eastern, southern and central United States, characterized by plant-raising (except possibly in its Initial Phase), by elongated globular clay pots (with cord-roughened exteriors, pointed bottoms, and incised line and punctate decoration), hamlets or small villages (except in the Classic Phase), with flint spearheads (but no arrowheads except in Final Phase).

WRAP-AROUND-SKIRT: A rectangular piece of clothing made of skin, fur, or cloth worn by Hopewellian and Middle Mississippi women. It was wrapped around the body from the waist to the knees or below and was secured at the top by a belt or other means.

YUMA POINTS: Chipped spearheads of various general shapes including leaf-shaped forms, without channeling.

BIBLIOGRAPHY

	ADVANCED (WOODLAND) PHASE
1951	Cole, F. C. et al in *The Baumer Focus*, in KINCAID, A PREHISTORIC ILLINOIS METROPOLIS, pp. 184-210, University of Chicago, Chicago (Baumer Subculture).
1951	Maxwell, Moreau S. *The Woodland Cultures in Southern Illinois*, pp. 232-243. Beloit College, Beloit, Wisconsin (Baumer Subculture).
1951	*Ibid.*, pp. 78-183 (Crab Orchard Subculture).
Tennessee	
1922	Harrington, M. R. *Cherokee and Earliest Remains on Upper Tennessee River*, INDIAN NOTES AND MONOGRAPHS, No. 24, New York (Round Grave People or Baumer Subculture).
1952	Kneberg, Madeline. *The Tennessee Area* in Griffin, Ed., ARCHAEOLOGY OF THE EASTERN UNITED STATES, p. 192 and Fig. 102., University of Chicago, Chicago (Round Grave, Upper Valley or Baumer).
	ARCHAIC PHASE
1950	Deuel, Thorne. *Man's Venture in Culture*, STORY OF ILLINOIS SERIES, No. 6, pp. 5-12, Illinois State Museum, Springfield.
1957	Deuel, Thorne, *The Modoc Shelter*, REPORT OF INVESTIGATIONS, No. 7, Springfield, revised and reprinted from *Natural History*, October, 1957, pp. 400-405 (Simple and Medial).
1956	Fowler, Melvin L. and Winters, Howard. *Modoc Rock Shelter, Preliminary Report*, REPORT OF INVESTIGATIONS, No. 4, Illinois State Museum, Springfield. (Simple and Medial).
1957	Fowler, Melvin L. *Ferry Site, Hardin County, Illinois*, SCIENTIFIC PAPERS SERIES, Vol. VIII, No. 1, Illinois State Museum, Springfield. (Terminal Subculture).
1950	Titterington, P. F. *Some Non-Pottery Sites in the St. Louis Area* in ILLINOIS STATE ARCHAEOLOGICAL JOURNAL, N.S. Vol. I, pp. 19-31 (Terminal Subculture).

Tennessee	
1947	Lewis, T. M. N. and Kneberg, Madeline. *The Archaic Horizon in Western Tennessee*, The University of Tennessee, Knoxville (Eva focus or subculture).
United States generally	
1957	Wormington, H. M. *Ancient Man in North America*, POPULAR SERIES, No. 4, 4th Edition, revised, Denver (Archaic and Paleo-Indian Assemblages).
CLASSIC (HOPEWELLIAN) PHASE	
1937	Cole, F. C. and Deuel, Thorne. *Rediscovering Illinois*, pp. 130-191. University of Chicago, Chicago.
1952	Deuel, Thorne, Ed. *Hopewellian Communities*, SCIENTIFIC PAPERS SERIES, Vol. V, Illinois State Museum, Springfield.
1957	Fowler, Melvin L. *Rutherford Mound, Hardin County, Illinois*, SCIENTIFIC PAPERS SERIES, Vol. VII, No. 1, Illinois State Museum, Springfield.
MIDDLE (MISSISSIPPI) PHASE	
Cahokia Subculture	
1937	Cole, F. C. and Deuel, Thorne. *Rediscovering Illinois*, pp. 75-94, 111-125, 127, University of Chicago, Chicago.
1928	Moorehead, W. K. *The Cahokia Mounds*, University of Illinois, BULLETIN, Vol. 26, No. 4, Urbana.
1939	Simpson, A. M. *The Kingston Village Site*, Peoria Academy of Science, Peoria. (Privately printed.)
1952	Smith, Hale G. *The Crable Site, Fulton County, Illinois*, ANTHROPOLOGY PAPERS No. 7, University of Michigan, Ann Arbor.
1938	Titterington, P. F. *The Cahokia Mound Group and Its Village Site Materials*, St. Louis. (Privately printed.)
Cahokia Subculture (Wisconsin)	
1933	Barrett, S. A. *Ancient Aztalan*, BULL. PUBLIC MUSEUM OF MILWAUKEE, Vol. 13.
Cumberland Subculture	

1951	Cole, F. C. et al. *Kincaid, A Prehistoric Illinois Metropolis*, pp. 29-164, 293-366, University of Chicago, Chicago.
	Cumberland Subculture (Tennessee)
1928	Myer, William, Ed. *Two Prehistoric Villages in Middle Tennessee*, 41st ANNUAL REPORT, BUREAU OF AMERICAN ETHNOLOGY, pp. 485-614, Washington.
	Cumberland Subculture (Kentucky)
1929	Webb, William S. and Funkhouser, W. D. *The Williams Site in Christian County, Kentucky*, UNIVERSITY OF KENTUCKY REPORTS IN ANTHROPOLOGY AND ARCHAEOLOGY, Vol. I, No. 1, pp. 5-23 followed by 36 figs., Lexington.
	**PALEO-INDIAN PHASE**
1954	Kleine, Harold K. *A Remarkable Paleo-Indian Site in Alabama* in TEN YEARS OF THE TENNESSEE ARCHAEOLOGIST, Lewis and Kneberg, Ed., reprinted from TENNESSEE ARCHAEOLOGIST, 1954.
1951	Smail, William. *Some Early Projectile Points from the St. Louis Area*, in ILLINOIS STATE ARCHAEOLOGICAL JOURNAL, N. S., Vol. II, No. 1, pp. 11-16.
1957	Wormington, H. M. *Ancient Man in North America*, POPULAR SERIES, No. 4, 4th Edition, revised, Denver.
	**UPPER (MISSISSIPPI) PHASE**
1927	Langford, George, Sr. *The Fisher Mound Group, Successive Aboriginal Occupations near the Mouth of the Illinois River*, in AMERICAN ANTHROPOLOGIST, Vol. XXIX, No. 3, pp. 153-206, Menasha.
	**FINAL WOODLAND**
	Bluff Subculture
1935	Titterington, P. F. *Certain Bluff Mounds of Western Jersey County, Illinois* in AMERICAN ANTIQUITY, Vol. I, No. 1, pp. 6-46.
1943	Titterington, P. F. *The Jersey County, Illinois, Bluff Culture*, in AMERICAN ANTIQUITY, Vol. IX, No. 2, pp. 240-245.
	Effigy Mound Subculture (Wisconsin)

1932	Barrett, S. A. and Skinner, Alanson. *Certain Mound and Village Sites of Shawano and Oconto Counties, Wisconsin*, BULL. PUBLIC MUSEUM OF MILWAUKEE, Vol. 10, No. 5, Milwaukee.
1928	McKern, W. C. *The Neal and McClaughry Mound Groups*, BULL. PUBLIC MUSEUM OF MILWAUKEE, Vol. 3, No. 3, Milwaukee.
1933	Nash, Philleo. *The Excavation of the Ross Mound Group I*, BULL. PUBLIC MUSEUM OF MILWAUKEE, Vol. 16, No. 1.
1956	Rowe, Chandler. *The Effigy Mound Culture of Wisconsin*, MILWAUKEE PUBLIC MUSEUM PUBLICATIONS IN ANTHROPOLOGY, No. 3.
Lewis Subculture	
1951	Cole, F. C. et al. *The Lewis Focus* in KINCAID, A PREHISTORIC ILLINOIS METROPOLIS, pp. 165-183, University of Chicago, Chicago.
Raymond Subculture	
1952	Maxwell, Moreau S. *Archaeology of the Lower Ohio Valley* in Griffin, Ed., COLE ANNIVERSARY VOLUME, ARCHAEOLOGY OF THE EASTERN UNITED STATES, pp. 186-187 and Fig. 100, University of Chicago, Chicago.
1951	Maxwell, Moreau S. *The Woodland Cultures in Southern Illinois*, pp. 78-172, 194-211, Beloit College, Beloit, Wisconsin.
Stone Vault Subculture	
1935	Thurber, O. D. *New Type of Burial Mound Near Quincy* in TRANSACTIONS ILLINOIS STATE ACADEMY OF SCIENCE, Springfield, Vol. XXVIII, No. 2, pp. 67-68.
1910	Fowke, Gerard. *Antiquities of Central and Southeastern Missouri*, BULL. BUREAU OF AMERICAN ETHNOLOGY, No. 37, Washington.
Tampico Subculture	
1937	Cole, F. C. and Deuel, Thorne. *Rediscovering Illinois*, pp. 191-198, University of Chicago, Chicago.

ILLINI TRIBES	
1934	Pease, Theodore Calvin and Werner, Raymond C. THE FRENCH FOUNDATIONS, 1680-1693 (*Memoirs of De Gannes* by Sieur Deliette) pp. 302-395, Springfield, Illinois.
1958	Temple, Wayne C. *Historic Tribes, Part 2 of Indian Villages of the Illinois Country* by Sara J. Tucker and Wayne Temple, SCIENTIFIC PAPERS SERIES, Vol. II, Illinois State Museum, Springfield.
INITIAL (WOODLAND) PHASE	
1937	Cole, F. C. and Deuel, Thorne. *Rediscovering Illinois* (Red Ochre, pp. 57-69; Black Sand, pp. 69-75, 136-149; Morton, pp. 39-46, 126, 128-130; 102-104, 106-108), University of Chicago, Chicago.

CULTURAL CHARACTERISTICS OF ARCHAEOLOGICAL UNITS

ARCHAEOLOGICAL UNITS		
ARTIFACTS[20]	RECONSTRUCTION OF ECONOMIC AND SOCIAL FEATURES	RECONSTRUCTION OF RELIGIOUS, ARTISTIC, AND RECREATIONAL FEATURES
PALEO-INDIAN PHASE 50,000(?)-8000 B.C.(?)		
Narrow leaf-shaped spearheads Folsom points Clovis points Stone hammer (?) Flint scrapers (?) Personal ornaments (?)	Thrusting weapons Simple family (?) Lineage in male line (?) Big game hunting Roving habits following herd Temporary camps Energy sources for labor, travel and transportation wholly human	Religion based on spirits, mana and on the chief game species hunted (?)
ARCHAIC PHASE 8000-2500 B.C.		
Stone hammers, rough or pitted Broad barbed flint spearheads Flint dartheads Flint scrapers Flint awls Chipped choppers Spearthrower (atlatl) weights	Projectile weapon Hunting of deer and small mammals and collecting edible plants, clams, etc. Technologies: flint-chipping, pecking, grinding and polishing of stone, grinding and polishing bone, boring bone and stone with flint drills and with tube, sand and water,	Belief in friendly and ancestral spirits, in mana and in revelation by vision or dream Sacred tradition ("mythology") The shaman— intercessor with spirits and healer of sick— magic medicines Fertility ceremonies— to insure abundant game and to

Grooved stone axes (ground)	making string (from hides and [?] plant-fibers), weaving (?), basket-making (?)	perpetuate sacred traditions
Ground stone celts		Recreational activities and creative arts practiced chiefly in connection with religious ceremonies
Chipped flint digging tools (hoes)	Dog the only domesticated animal	
	Marriage	
Small area settlement sites in the open	Family	Funeral rites for all deceased tribal members
	Extended family or lineage	
Rock shelters	"Independent" local groups	Socially important persons on death given special care and preparation for burial, and possibly buried in a specially selected place
Post holes in line		
	Windbreaks or flimsy shelters	
Necklaces and pendants		
	Family hunting territory	
Plummets		Mourning period for dead
Copper tools	Rotating hamlet	
Dog bones	Non-political tribe	Food and grave offerings left especially for important dead
Bone-awls	"Family-type" social control	
Whet- or abrading stones		
	Puberty rites (Initiation ceremonies)	
Bannerstones (with cylindrical hole)	Tribal elders and temporary headmen	
Flexed burials in Medial and Terminal subculture	Insignia possibly as social acceptance of personal achievement, or as family crest	

INITIAL (WOODLAND) PHASE 1500-500 B.C.

Elongated globular pots with pointed (conoidal) bases	Probably very similar to Archaic	Very similar to Archaic
		Dog graves in burial mounds
	Copper breastplate or gorgets	
Copper ornaments		

Burial mounds and cemeteries	Socially important persons buried in mounds (?)	
ADVANCED (WOODLAND) PHASE 1000(?)-100(?) B.C.		
Numerous storage pits containing acorn and hickory nut remains Medium-sized settlement sites Post holes outlining a square area Post holes outlining a circular or oval area Flat-bottomed flaring-walled Woodland pots ("flower pots") Polished stone gorgets Burials in settlement sites	Storage of acorns, nuts and seeds Larger population concentrations of perhaps a 100 or 150 persons Semi- to permanent log dwellings, logs upright Possibly insignia or badges of leadership or individual prowess	Religion probably transitional between Archaic and plant-raising types
CLASSIC (WOODLAND) PHASE [HOPEWELLIAN] 500 B.C.-500 A.D.		
Chipped limonite hoes Charred maize kernels and cobs (and in Ohio, beans and squash seeds)	Planting-raising economy supplemented by hunting and collecting Crops: Maize, beans, squash, tobacco	Probably a formalized religion based on the chief food plant, maize Regularly appointed priests The priest probably wore feather robes

Cloth and feather cloth remains	Weaving of cloth, basket- and mat-making	and insignia of rank and position
Basketry, matting and colored textile impressions	Clothing: Wrap-around-skirt for women, breech cloth for men, supplemented by robes in cold weather, feather cloth robes in ceremonies. Mocassins for women and probably for men.	Religion probably included ceremonies connected with plant- or maize-raising
Marine shell vessels		Deities or gods with special powers related to food-raising, etc.
Tortoise shell dishes		The spring or planting festival
River mussel shell spoons with "handles"	Large villages (or clusters of villages) as well as small settlements	The green corn or first fruits festival
Excellent polished black and painted pottery with occasional variation of form—shallow bowls, beakers, effigy and globular shapes		The harvest festival and perhaps minor festivals revolving about the deer
	The wigwam (for lower classes?)	High-ranking priests were probably of the highest caste and their bodies given special care on death, elaborate funeral ceremonies and burial in the tomb chambers of mounds, with tribal mourning
	Possibly log cabin dwellings for highest social class, logs laid horizontal as in tomb chambers	
	Rise of wealth, rich and extensive trade	
A coarser duty Woodland ware with elongated bodies and pointed or flattened bases	Dug-out boats (?)	
	Two or three social classes seem to be indicated by burial customs	Beautiful pipes either with or without long wooden items probably figured largely in the religious ceremonies
Large areas with village refuse and numerous mounds	Chiefs—a political form of government, with some of the clans, possibly bear, wolverine and bobcat, predominant in certain areas	
Post holes outlining an oval or circular area (rare)		Shamans probably still practiced the healing art (and black magic). They probably used herbals instead of mineral medicines

Pottery statuettes showing dress and ornaments worn	A tribe organized either politically or into clans with subsidiary districts or villages and political or clan chiefs.	High development of art in pottery, ceramic, copper and stone sculpture, in engraving on bone in personal adornment and technological expertness
Jewelry of copper, silver, meteoric iron, cut and polished shell beads, small marine shells, bears teeth sometimes set with copper, pearls or colorful stones, etc.	Chiefs may have worn deer antler headdresses.	
	Chiefs probably wore feather headdresses, feather cloth robes, mantles embroidered with pearls shells and cut shell beads, and other insignia of office.	
Ear ornaments of copper, etc.	Tomb chambers probably for chiefs with relatives and retainers slain to accompany them	
Marine shells from south Atlantic and Gulf Coasts of United States		
Mica from North Carolina	Chief person in tomb sometimes woman (May indicate matrilineal descent or simply ranking woman of highest caste)	
Obsidian from Wyoming (?)		
Copper from Lake Superior region	Maxillary (jaw) pendants worn maybe as trophies of war and hunt, or to indicate clan of a chief (?)	
Galena from northwestern Illinois	Doubtless the pipe served (as it did later) as a safe conduct to visiting officials, travellers and traders, and a signature and seal to important	
Native pearls from river clams		
Gorgets of stone, shell and		

copper (breastplates)	agreements whether economic, political or intertribal	
Pearls and ground shell beads distributed over the torso of skeleton		
Deer antlers near human skull in grave		
Cut maxillaries (more rarely mandibles) of bear or man on skeletons as if worn as pendants		
Cassis madagascarensis shell vessels		
Copper hatchets and adzes etc.		
Platform type tobacco pipes		
Medium to large "dome-shaped" burial mounds enclosing		
Log (rarely stone) tomb chambers		
Bundle burials and ossuaries in mounds with central tomb (northern Illinois)		

Cemeteries near mounds (southern Illinois)		
Bodies buried generally in extended position rarely flexed and often accompanied by pots, weapons and artistic products		
"Pipes of Pan"		
Beautifully chipped broad spearheads of special subtypes		
Effigy dagger with sheath made from bears' teeth		
FINAL (WOODLAND) PHASE 200(?)-1000 A.D.		
Boatstones and bar "amulets" L-shaped pipe, long-stemmed Crude flint arrowheads Flexed and semi-flexed skeletons in mound graves and tomb chambers Except for above, much like Initial Phase	Spear and spearthrower still the chief weapon, weights tied (?) to spearthrower Small hamlets Bow and arrow known but as yet ineffective as a practical weapon Otherwise very similar to Initial Phase	Religion probably with shamans rather than priests and a mixture of Initial and Classic Phase religious beliefs and practices and superstitions Some considerable sanctity probably still attached to tobacco, tobacco smoke and the pipe Shamans undoubtedly still practiced the healing arts (as well as black magic) and

		possibly simple religious rites
MIDDLE (MISSISSIPPI) PHASE 1000-1500 A.D.		
Hoes of chipped flint and numerous digging tools

Charred maize kernels and cobs

Large settlement areas with flat-topped pyramidal mounds, with cabin remains on summits, surrounded by palisade remains in low ridges of earth

Post holes and/or trenches outlining rectangular house floors. Fired clay from wattle and daub structure, burned house with charred thatch, timbers, rafters, mats, etc.

Fire pits or fireplaces within house

Fine polished black and painted wares | Intensive maize growing with other crops supplemented by hunting

Repeating weapon (bow and arrows)

Energy sources for labor and transportation still entirely human

The finer pottery and burials in mounds and cemeteries may reflect class differences. The extension of the pottery shapes from the fine black ware to the less decorative service ware may indicate an improvement of lower class conditions over those in Hopewellian times

Clothing much like Hopewellian in general styles

Large villages, small cities and small villages

Large centers or cities had temples and tribal officers' cabins on flat-topped mounds, and were protected by palisades and/or mud walls | Religious ceremonial centers or cities existed to which outlying smaller village populations journeyed for religious festivals

Priesthood with appropriate dress and regalia

Temples or sacred groves for worship

Religion with deities having special powers relating to maize-growing. Veneration or worship of ancestors

Spring, first fruits, and harvest festivals

Tobacco smoke, tobacco pipes used in ceremonies as incense offerings

Athletic games form part of ceremonies

Shamans still exist but chiefly for healing, etc. as among Hopewellians

High-ranking officials and priests buried in graves in mounds. Usual preparation of body, burial, mourning periods, elaborated |

with globular and flattened globular bodies, in many shapes—water bottles, shallow bowls, beakers, ollas or jars and effigy forms	Dwellings semi- to permanent, with rectangular floors, vaulted or gabled roofs of thatch, walls consisting of vertical posts, wattle and daub construction, covered inside and out with mats, sometimes possibly bark-covered. Cabin remains numerous.	proportionately to the rank of the deceased. Art well developed Games of chance were probably known and played
An excellent, dull-gray service ware with similar varieties of shapes		
An excellent storage ware of medium to large size, chiefly globular in form	Dug-out boats (?) Wealth considerable. Trade in fewer materials than in Hopewellian	
Busycon, marginella, olivella shells from south Atlantic and Gulf Coasts	Two or three social classes present in population as in Hopewellian	
Copper from Lake Superior region	Probably a political government with tribal and war chiefs and village chiefs. Head tribal chief may have been chief priest also, or a member of his family may have filled later office. War chief probably also member of ruling caste (as among Natchez). Other war chiefs probably of other classes, rank based on their past deeds	
Busycon dippers and drinking cups		
L-shaped pipe ("equal armed" and and medium long-stemmed varieties)		
Massive effigy stone pipes	Tribal and war chief. In some villages, village chief possibly	

Skeletons, in extended positions, (distributed) in single and multiple graves throughout mounds and in cemeteries

Pottery Vessels, weapon heads, jewelry, and polished stone discoidals, etc. associated with skeletons

Shell gorgets engraved with realistic and conventional designs

Repoussee copper eagle gorgets or plaques

Copper sheeted ornaments and jewelry of pottery, bone, shell, wood and leather

Polished stone disks or "wheels"

Ground and squared astragalus bone of deer and elk | had dwellings on pyramid tops

Headdresses, probably with feathers, and regalia, including feather-cloth robes were probably worn on tribal occasions of importance

Calumet pipe doubtless served as safe conduct to travellers and visiting officials, as seal and signature to important agreements. Effigy stone pipes may have been Middle Phase calumet pipe since it had to be smoked with a stem

War parties still of simple or no organization except leader and followers, object to take prisoners but not territory | |

UPPER PHASE 1100(?)-1600 A.D.		
Note: These are fringe groups in relation to Middle and Lower phases, living in more wooded regions perhaps, where game was especially abundant and topography less favorable to plant-raising by a backward culture and where the social impetus for high cultural development was largely lacking	A hunting-collecting economy with plant-raising probably in garden-like plots	A religion based on plant-raising but probably with considerable emphasis on chief animals hunted.
	Large and small villages	Sacred groves and shrines, possibly temples in some of larger villages
	A social development similar to but simpler than the Middle Phase, probably a combination of Woodland and Mississippi elements	No pyramidal mounds
		Dead buried in mounds and in cemeteries
Artifacts are a mixture of Woodland and Mississippi types		
Generally a single pottery ware with both elongated and globular pots is characteristic and there is little other specialization of form		

CONTACT PHASE (ILLINI) 1673-1833 A.D.

Note: The artifacts of all tribes in the historic period probably became gradually much the same regardless of their prior cultural status due to deterioration of native technology and trading of furs for European tools, weapons, cloth, etc. Arrowheads of chipped flint, and native-made of European copper, brass or iron Numerous trade articles such as glass beads, gun parts, copper or brass kettles, bottles for wine, olives, etc. and other objects of European production Native stone molds and cast lead balls (for guns) and native	Bow and arrows preferred in war because they could be discharged more rapidly than gun could be loaded and fired. Guns and ammunition often not available Little knowledge of proper care of guns, and no attempt to manufacture guns and powder, or iron knives, copper kettles, etc. Society largely disorganized, prestige of chiefs largely a matter of personal prowess and reputation with some regard for earlier methods of appointment and succession.	Religion practiced by a fraction of tribe but falling into dispute without adequate substitute Probably appointment and succession of priests more or less regular and based on earlier customs.

chipped gun flints		
Rectangular L-shaped ("Siouan type") pipes of catlinite and other stone. Micmac pipes after 1700.		

FOOTNOTES

[5] All dates, even those determined by radiocarbon methods, should be taken as only roughly approximate.

[6] These dates and those given hereafter refer to the earliest and latest sites known in Illinois for the cultures under consideration. Although supported by radiocarbon dating methods, they are only approximate. Undoubtedly also cultures in one area disappeared while they continued to flourish in another part of the state or in other states.

[7] Generally speaking, each succeeding higher culture in the area made most of the tool and weapon types of their predecessors, adding certain improvements and sometimes new types. The Archaic people used flint scrapers, chipped flint choppers, and native cobblestone hammers as had the Paleo-Indians. The narrow-bladed spearheads were occasionally made but the fluting or channel is practically always lacking. Polished stone forms, possibly the spearthrower, were new inventions in Archaic times.

[8] In the page that follows a tentative reconstruction of the less tangible customs of these people will be presented, based on a study of several tribes now or recently in the Archaic status. The Archaic culture as used in this paper refers to those tribes who lived mainly by hunting, supplemented to a degree by collecting native edible plant foods. They are distinguished here from other peoples of the Stone Age or non-farming stage—from Big Game Hunters on the one hand (none of whom exist today) and on the other, from Food Stores, who were able by one means or another to store food over one or more seasons and so establish more or less fixed homes. The peoples recently living in the Archaic status include the native tribes of Central and Coastal Australia, the Tasmanians, the Andaman Island tribes, the Terra del Fuegians, the African Bushmen and a number of others.

[9] The Initial Woodland in Illinois is usually considered to consist of three cultural divisions or units, the Black Sand, the

Red Ochre and the Morton. The only known Red Ochre sites are mounds which undoubtedly are the burial places of important personages of a cultural group whose campsites and artifact assemblages have not as yet been identified as such. The graves yield a number of artifact types that are identical with those found in Black Sand villages. It is possible the Red Ochre mounds belong to the Black Sand people and that the mounds and special burial customs may have been continued into or adopted by the Morton cultural group and served still later as a framework for the highly elaborated Hopewellian funeral practices.

[10]The narrow-bladed leaf-shaped spearhead, well-chipped and without fluting, reminiscent of the general Yuma, Folsom and Clovis shape, are found in the Red Ochre subculture and are worthy of note. This type appears rarely in campsites but occurs in relatively large numbers in mounds. Profuse amounts of red ochre are found in graves as in Terminal Archaic (Titterington focus) in western Illinois. Copper ornaments may indicate Wisconsin (Old Copper Culture) influence.

[11]The Poole village (Pike County) is dated 550 B.C. and the Wilson Mound (White County) about 89 B.C. The Poole village appears to have been occupied from 550 B.C. to 200 A.D.

[12]Civilization, as used in this paper, signifies exhaustive exploitation of the natural resources and accompanying significant elaborations of the social and spiritual aspects (as exemplified by ceremonies, regalia, insignia, art and extensive architectural structures), accomplished by means of specialization of the existing tools and technologies, with or without fundamental inventive developments. Artisans of the Initial and Final Woodland cultures seem to have practiced all the crafts employed by Hopewellians but failed to produce the beautiful chipped spearheads, "pipes of pan", excellent sculpture in stone and pottery, etching in bone, the extensive earthworks and the mounds with timbered burial chambers. Perhaps some additional stimuli—the introduction of maize or the intensification of its cultivation, a satisfying new religion with stirring ceremonies together with intergroup

competition—gave the spiritual impetus that produced the Hopewellian fluorescence.

[13]Specialization was foreshadowed in the Red Ochre culture but the small total of grave offerings discovered to date fail to demonstrate any greater leisure than occurs at favorable times among any simple hunting people.

[14]An early subculture termed Old Village preceding the generally known Middle Mississippi (Trappist or Bean Pot) period has been proposed on the strength of stratification at the Cahokia village near East St. Louis. Although this appears logically sound, the evidence has not been published and no pure Old Village site has yet been found and reported upon.

[15]Except where noted as based directly on archaeological evidence, the broad cultural features suggested in the rest of this section, are inferred from similar customs found generally among tribes in the plant-raising status without food-draft animals. The results were derived by the writer from a study of anthropological reports of the following tribes or groups of tribes: Polynesians, Delawares, Natchez (and their neighbors) and the western Pueblo Indians. The Pueblos, in their social, political and religious customs and institutions have been for seven hundred years in a transitional status between the Archaic hunters (or possibly "food storers") and a "fully-developed" plant-raising stage.

[16]The archaeological evidence for this section is chiefly from *The Fisher Mound Group*, etc. by George Langford in the AMERICAN ANTHROPOLOGY, Vol. XXIX, No. 3, pp. 153-205 (July-September, 1927).

[17]These Indians called themselves Ilini (pronounced Il´-i-nee) or Illini signifying "man," in the plural Illiniwek, "the men." The French dropped the -iwek and substituted their own ending whence the name Illinois by which they were generally known thereafter. In this booklet Illini will be generally used to designate these tribes, their culture and language to avoid confusion with other tribes who, like the

Sauk, Fox, Kickapoo, Potawatomi, and Miami, have occupied parts of the state and are sometimes called Illinois Indians.

[18] Information given on historic tribes is from notes and manuscript assembled by Dr. Wayne C. Temple.

[19] The term *calumet*, originally applied to the stem of the tobacco pipe, is now generally used to designate the pipe and stem. "It is fashioned from a red stone, polished like marble, and bored in such a manner that one end serves as a receptacle for the tobacco, while the other fits into the stem; this is a stick two feet long, as thick as an ordinary cane, and bored through the middle. It is ornamented with the heads and necks of various birds, whose plumage is very beautiful. To these they also add large feathers—red, green, and other colors—wherewith the whole is adorned. They have a great regard for it...." (R. G. Thwaites, ed., *The Jesuit Relations*, Vol. LIX, p. 131.) The war calumet differed from that of peace and was decorated with red feathers. See Fig. 34, A.

[20] Artifact types having once appeared are likely to appear again in subsequent culture even though rare or even lacking in some intervening assemblages (e.g. necklaces of anculosa beads of similarly ground [snail] shells found from Medial Archaic through Middle Phase; grooved axes from Medial Archaic to Mississippi but rare or lacking in most subcultures and cultures except Archaic and Initial Woodland). On account of unwieldiness of complete accumulative lists only new artifact types when they first appear will be recorded here. Exceptions: 1) the name of an artifact entered as probably present (indicated by a following ?) will be repeated in the first subsequent culture in which definite evidence for it has been reported and 2) when an artifact once reported assumes a new form or presumably takes on a new significance (e.g. Archaic hoe becomes a tool of the plant-raisers in Classic and Middle Phases), it will appear again in the text.

www.ingramcontent.com/pod-product-compliance
Ingram Content Group UK Ltd.
Pitfield, Milton Keynes, MK11 3LW, UK
UKHW031337260325
456749UK00002B/366